T0319062

Cambridge Elements ≡

Elements in the Philosophy of Religion
edited by
Yujin Nagasawa
University of Birmingham

GOD AND ABSTRACT OBJECTS

Einar Duenger Bøhn
University of Agder

CAMBRIDGE
UNIVERSITY PRESS

CAMBRIDGE
UNIVERSITY PRESS

University Printing House, Cambridge CB2 8BS, United Kingdom

One Liberty Plaza, 20th Floor, New York, NY 10006, USA

477 Williamstown Road, Port Melbourne, VIC 3207, Australia

314–321, 3rd Floor, Plot 3, Splendor Forum, Jasola District Centre,
New Delhi – 110025, India

79 Anson Road, #06–04/06, Singapore 079906

Cambridge University Press is part of the University of Cambridge.

It furthers the University's mission by disseminating knowledge in the pursuit of
education, learning, and research at the highest international levels of excellence.

www.cambridge.org
Information on this title: www.cambridge.org/9781108457446
DOI: 10.1017/9781108558112

First published 2019

A catalogue record for this publication is available from the British Library.

ISBN 978-1-108-45744-6 Paperback
ISSN 2399-5165 (online)
ISSN 2515-9763 (print)

Cambridge University Press has no responsibility for the persistence or accuracy of
URLs for external or third-party internet websites referred to in this publication
and does not guarantee that any content on such websites is, or will remain,
accurate or appropriate.

God and Abstract Objects

Elements in the Philosophy of Religion

DOI: 10.1017/9781108558112
First published online: July 2019

Einar Duenger Bøhn
University of Agder

Author for correspondence: Einar Duenger Bøhn, einar.d.bohn@uia.no

Abstract: Some believe that there is a God who is the source of all things; and some believe that there are necessarily existing abstract objects. But can one believe both these things? That is the question of this Element. First, Einar Duenger Bøhn clarifies the concepts involved and the problem that arises from believing in both God and abstract objects. Second, he presents and discusses the possible kinds of solution to that problem. Third, he discusses a new kind of solution to the problem, according to which reality is most fundamentally made of information.

Keywords: philosophy of religion, God, abstract objects, grounding, information

ISBNs: 9781108457446 (PB), 9781108558112 (OC)
ISSNs: 2399-5165 (online), 2515-9763 (print)

Contents

Introduction

Some believe that there is an eternal, aspatial, necessary, and concrete personal being worthy of worship who created all things apart from hirself, i.e. that there is a God. Some believe that there are eternal, aspatial, necessary, and abstract objects, that there are, e.g., mathematical objects, properties, or propositions (the contents of our thoughts). Roughly, the question of this book is: Can we coherently believe both that there is such a God and that there are such abstract objects at the same time? That is what I will call the problem of God and abstract objects.

In section 1, I explain the concepts involved, especially that of God and abstract objects, as well as the main problem that arises, if the concepts are instantiated. In section 2, I sketch and discuss the various kinds of solutions, in the order of plausibility, ending with the most plausible solution. In section 3, I nonetheless explore the option of rejecting one of the basic presuppositions for the problem to arise in the first place, namely that the fundamental ontology consists of objects and properties. I suggest that it consists of pure information that can be coded in different ways. Such a position carries great promise to solve the problem of God and abstract objects.

Before we get started, I should warn the reader of several things. First, I will argue neither for nor against the existence of neither God nor abstract objects. This Element is mostly about the problem that arises from their supposed joint existence and possible solutions to that problem. I do consider the option of rejecting either God or abstract objects but mostly for taxonomic purposes.

Second, I pay no attention to the history of philosophy. For example, I do not discuss Augustine, Aquinas, or Descartes, even though some of their works are highly relevant to the problem at hand. This is mostly owing to limited space but also, of course, my personal interests and expertise (or bias).

Third, what follows is not so much a traditional introduction as a highly opinionated, somewhat argued overview of the problem of God and abstract objects. I introduce and discuss the problem in the way I find to be the most clearheaded and interesting. I also spend the third section discussing a new kind of solution to the problem. Yet, given the space allotted, I must leave many issues underdeveloped and unresolved, so I take many stands as I go along and I leave this section highly speculative, more a suggestion for future research than a clear position possible to accept at this point.

Fourth, I pay no attention to religious texts. In general, I distinguish between systematic theology, which deals with particular religious texts, and the philosophy of religion, which deals with much more general religious problems. The way I treat the problem of God and abstract objects in what follows is as a general problem in the philosophy of religion, not in systematic theology. (I therefore also use the gender-neutral pronoun "hir" for God rather than the more theologically traditional "his." Get used to it!)

1 The Problem

So what is the problem of God and abstract objects more exactly? It turns out that there are many problems but, at the most general level, the problem is simply how to reconcile a certain notion of God with a certain notion of abstract objects. There seems to be a problem with how both kinds of objects can coexist in the sense we normally tend to think of them. There are reasons to use both notions but they are mutually inconsistent, so they cannot both have an extension; or at least so it seems.

In this first section, I will specify the notion of God involved (section 1.1), the notion of abstract objects involved (section 1.2), and, finally, the inconsistencies and problems that arise from their supposed coexistence (section 1.3).

1.1 God

In general, I will understand God as a personal being worthy of worship, which might in turn require a maximal level of collective greatness with respect to all hir features (see Nagasawa, 2008, 2017; see also Bohn, 2012). Yet, in order for the present inconsistencies and problems of God and abstract objects to arise, we must assume some more specific theses about God.

First, we must assume that God is the first cause and fundamental ground of all things distinct from God hirself. This is what I have elsewhere called the thesis of *Divine Foundationalism* (DF; see Bohn, 2018b). By "distinct," I here simply mean nonidentical. By "first cause and ultimate ground," I here mean that God is the *source* – both diachronically and synchronically – of all things distinct from God. That is, everything distinct from God originates in or from God.

Second, we must also assume the thesis of *Divine Aseity* (DA), according to which God is uncreated, self-sufficient, and existentially independent of all things distinct from hirself. Note that while DF entails DA, and hence, by assuming DF, we thereby also assume DA, DA does not entail DF. Something can be uncreated, self-sufficient, and existentially independent without being the first cause or fundamental ground of anything. Abstract objects, in particular mathematical objects like the pure set-theoretical hierarchy, might be a case in point. They might be uncreated, exist in their own right, independently of all other things, but be the source of nothing else.

Third, we will assume the thesis of *Divine Sovereignty* (DS), according to which everything distinct from God is under God's creative control. DS is thus related to God's supposed omnipotence. It is up to God to create, change, or eliminate all things distinct from God hirself. Rejecting DS is restricting God's powers.

Fourth, we will also assume the thesis of *Divine Necessity* (DN; see Bohn, 2017), according to which God must exist in the sense that, metaphysically speaking, God cannot possibly fail to exist (if God exists at all). DN is here not only claiming that for any possible way the world could have been some god or other exists in that possibility but rather that the one and only God could not have failed to exist no matter what. The theses of DF and DN are logically independent of each other.

Fifth, we will assume the thesis of *Divine Eternity* (DE), according to which God is eternal in the sense of being either of (the highest) infinite duration or atemporal ("outside of" time). DE is logically independent of all of DF, DA, DS, and DN.

Sixth, we will assume the thesis of *divine aspatiality* (DA_s), according to which God is aspatial in the sense that God is not bounded by space in the sense of being located somewhere, anywhere, or everywhere in our physical space. God transcends physical space. DA_S is logically independent of all the other above-mentioned theses.

Note that the first thesis, DF, is the most essential for the problem of God and abstract objects to arise. Yet, as we will see, the others will play important roles as well.

Finally, we will assume that God is a *concrete* being.[1] There is no agreed on definition of what it is to be concrete but two more plausible criteria are that it *obeys the law of excluded middle with respect to properties* and that it has *causal powers*. First, consider the criterion of the law of excluded middle with respect to properties (LEM_P). Something is said to obey LEM_P just in case, for any property F, it either has F or not-F; and it is neither the case that it has both F and not-F nor the case that it has neither F nor not-F. Anything concrete is thus *determinate* in all real respects. This notion of being determinate should be kept separate from any notion of vagueness, i.e. being determinate should here be kept separate from being nonvague. I take it vagueness is a matter of semantic indeterminacy or perhaps epistemic ignorance, never a worldly matter, but the notion of determinateness involved in LEM_P is a worldly matter. I thus take it that failing to obey LEM_P does not make something vague, only indeterminate in the specified sense of LEM_P.

---

[1] If God is abstract, we might get a similar but still different problem from the one we are interested in here. For a discussion of God being an abstract object, see Leftow (1990).

Intuitively, a *mathematical set* is an object that has members. Sets are individuated by their extensionality, which means that sets S and S* are the same just in case they share all their members. There are very, very many such sets out there. For example, there is the set having all the natural numbers as its members and there is the so-called singleton set having me as its sole member. There is also the empty set, which is the one and only set that has no members. Now, consider the set having me as its sole member. Is it located in exactly the same place I am? If there is no yes-or-no answer to that question, then, by LEM$_P$, that set is not concrete, like I am. Or consider the same set in relation to the set having you as its sole member. Which set is darker? One of us might be darker than the other but which one of our sets is darker than the other? Darkness does not seem to apply to sets. If there is no yes-or-no answer as to which of the two sets is darker than the other (including whether they are equally dark), then those sets are not concrete, like you and I are. In order to be concrete, you need to obey LEM$_P$.

A problem with this way of trying to understand concreteness is that there might not be a yes-or-no answer as to whether God is darker than me. Darkness might not apply to God at all; but still God is supposed to be concrete. Maybe concreteness is a matter of degree? More on that in section 1.2 and in section 3.4.

Second, consider the criterion of causal powers. Something is said to have causal powers only if it has the potential to bring about an effect in a causal chain. Consider again the singleton set having me as its sole member. Can it bring about an effect in a causal chain? I can bring about an effect in a causal chain but can my singleton set bring about an effect in a causal chain? If the answer is no, then, according to this criterion, it cannot be something concrete. Without any such potential to bring about some effect, it cannot be something concrete, like I am. In order to be concrete, you need to have causal powers.

It is worth noting that concrete things are also often said to be spatiotemporally located. I have a location in space and time, or space-time, but my mathematical set does not. But this criterion seems more problematic than the others. First of all, one might think that the set of me is just as spatiotemporally located as I am (it is where I am) but presumably one should still think it is not concrete. Second, for present purposes, God is aspatial (and perhaps atemporal), with no particular location in space (or time), but presumably God is still something concrete.

It is important to note that being concrete is not here assumed to be the same thing as being physical. Though it is notoriously hard to define "physical," it is usually assumed that all physical things are concrete but not thereby assumed that all concrete things are physical. In other words, there might be concrete things that are not physical. God is an example at hand: God is often supposed to be concrete but not physical. Other controversial examples might be some theoretical postulates in fundamental physics.[2] The idea is that, in order to be something concrete, you must be determinate and/or have causal powers to bring about causal chains but this should not be confused with the idea that all determinate things with causal powers are physical.

1.2 Abstract Objects

Abstract objects are often seen as a complement to or in opposition to concrete objects. That is, something is said to be *abstract* if and only if it is not concrete. For example, the two singleton sets considered in section 1.1 are, as opposed to you and me, not determinate with respect to which one is darker than the other, i.e. they do not obey LEM_P, so they are abstract rather than concrete. Likewise, they, by themselves, do not have the potential to enter into an ordinary causal chain, i.e. they are *causally inapt*, so they are, as opposed to you and me, abstract rather than concrete.

Some such distinction between abstract and concrete objects is often taken to be a fundamental distinction between two exhaustive and mutually exclusive fundamental kinds of thing. For example, Peter van Inwagen (2004) explicitly draws such a distinction (see also Cowling, 2017, s. 2.1). In order to draw the line between the two kinds, van Inwagen suggests that we can list a few paradigm cases of concrete and abstract objects (e.g. the Eiffel Tower and the ratio of one to zero, respectively) and then ask philosophers to group the rest of our terms in ordinary, philosophical, and scientific usage in either one of the two groups. He believes that there will then be substantial agreement among philosophers as to which term belongs in which group.

Now, even if van Inwagen is right about there being a substantial agreement as to which term belongs in which group, I am not sure what that is supposed to tell us, not to mention justify. History teaches us again and again that there is often much agreement about false things, even among experts, so a mere agreement is not in itself very impressive. And, after all, when you think about it some more, as Lewis (1986, pp. 81–86) did, the distinction *is* genuinely unclear and it is highly unclear what it is really doing for us (see also Burgess & Rosen, 1997). So, though philosophers might intuitively agree to some extent, that

---

[2] Being *physical* is often contrasted with being *mental*. All mental things are usually assumed to be concrete, though not all concrete things are assumed to be mental (though this is somewhat in tension with LEM_P being a necessary requirement for concreteness, since it might not to be the case that, e.g., for any two thoughts, one is darker than the other [though they seem to have causal powers]). To make things even worse, being *actual* is often contrasted with being *possible* but without thereby assuming that being actual coincides with being concrete or physical or that being possible coincides with being abstract or mental. Reality is complicated.

agreement is a shallow and shaky matter, not something we should rest our metaphysics on.

Of course, the fact that the line is hard to draw should already raise suspicions in connection with the very problem of this book, namely that of the relationship between God and abstract objects. But, nonetheless, as we know from very many other cases, an unclear distinction is not the same as no distinction. As van Inwagen correctly points out, we have some paradigm examples of abstract versus concrete things, e.g. a number versus a rock, and we have some illuminating but imperfect ways of trying to draw the distinction, which together give us an imperfect grasp of a rough distinction. The fact that there are some cases that blur this distinction is not by itself a good reason to conclude that there is no useful distinction there. It seems undoubtedly true that there is a distinction in kind between my body on the one hand and the set that has no members on the other. The former is what we call a concrete kind of thing and the latter is what we call an abstract kind of thing. Seemingly, the former obeys LEM_P and has causal powers, the latter does not. The fact that the singleton set that has my body as a member falls somewhere in between these two kinds of things does not make any of the two initial cases of the same kind but only the line between those two kinds not a fundamentally sharp line.

In fact, rather than concluding that there is no abstract/concrete distinction, perhaps we should conclude that the distinction is a rough matter of degree? I believe such a position deserves more attention than it has received. Presumably, I am not abstract but many of my essential properties are fairly abstract, e.g. my humanity. One might also think that my thoughts are more abstract than the various activities in my brain. So perhaps I am not fully concrete after all; at least I have some abstract elements, or even parts. But still the singleton set of me seems more abstract than I am. For example, while I, or at least my body, obey LEM_P and can enter into causal chains, making me as concrete as ordinary things get, my singleton set neither obeys LEM_P nor enters into causal chains, making it more abstract than concrete. But, even still, my singleton set does not seem as abstract as things get. For example, it might be just as spatially and temporally bounded as I am, as well as modally contingent as I am. That is, it seems located where I am, not only in actual space and time but in all possible worlds too. My singleton set thus seems to go where- and whenever I go, no matter what. But consider pure sets, in particular the empty set that has no members, found at the very bottom of the standard mathematical set-theoretical hierarchy. Sets, being individuated by their members, seem dependent on their members but the empty set has no members. As such, it seems spatially, temporally, and modally independent of anything but itself. Certainly, it does not depend on any concrete thing, neither spatially, temporally, nor modally. In fact, the empty set seems acausal, aspatial, atemporal, and amodal, not to mention inapt for many properties such as mass and color, making it as abstract as things get. Since the entire set-theoretical hierarchy can be built on top of the empty set, if all of pure mathematics can be reduced to the set-theoretical hierarchy (which is a live option in the philosophy of mathematics), the same goes for all pure mathematical objects: they are as abstract as things get – as opposed to you and me, or at least our bodies, which are as concrete as things get. So, even though the abstract/concrete distinction is unclear, there seems to be some such distinction there. Perhaps it is a continuous matter of degree from one extreme to another or perhaps it is a discrete matter of degree, with a finite set of steps between the fully abstract and the fully concrete.

A problem with the degree view is how to measure the degree. For example, what is most abstract, the singleton set of me or the proposition that I am me (or God, for that matter)? There seems no simple way to measure abstractness or concreteness. That might be a reason to stick with the sharp distinction between the abstract and the concrete after all. Personally, I am divided on the matter but believe the degree view deserves more attention before we settle on this. Though I will henceforth occasionally talk as if it is a matter of degree and discuss the matter further in section 3.4, no conclusion hinges on this. Our focus will, in any case, be on the relationship between God and the purely abstract objects there might be.

It is instructive to consider some more examples of concrete and abstract objects. While you and I are more concrete, many of our *properties* are more abstract. For example, we both instantiate the property of being human but, in order for us to both (genuinely) share that one and the same property, it must be something more abstract that can be instantiated more than once over at the same time, not something concrete that can only be instantiated once at a time. For an even more purely abstract property, consider the property of being self-identical. Unlike the property of being human, it seems temporally, spatially, and modally independent of not only humans but anything at all apart from itself. In terms of degree of abstractness, the property of being human is more like a set of concrete things (e.g. the set of all humans), while the property of being self-identical is more like the pure sets, uninfected by concreteness.

While you and I are more concrete, *propositions about us* are more abstract. For example, the proposition that we are human is something we can both express through thought or language. But, in order for us to both express that one and the same proposition (and hence for communication to be possible), it must be something more abstract that is publicly available to us, something that we can both grasp through thought or language, not something concrete isolated inside each our individual heads (see Frege, 1918).[3] For an even more purely abstract proposition, consider the proposition that everything is self-identical. Unlike the proposition that we are human, it seems temporally, spatially, and modally independent of not only the two of us and the property of humanity but anything at all apart from itself. In terms of degree of abstractness, the proposition that we are human is more like a set of concrete things (or the property of being human), while the proposition that everything is self-identical is more like the pure sets (or the property of being self-identical), uninfected by concreteness.

In short, the most abstract objects seem to be pure mathematical objects like pure sets, as well as what we might call pure logical properties and propositions. Such objects are not only uninfected by any concreteness (in the sense of, e.g., drastically failing LEM_P as well as being unable to participate in more or less ordinary causal chains)[4] but they are also aspatial, eternal, and necessary beings. Like God, their existence seems to be self-sufficient and independent of anything else.

It is such most purely abstract objects that should and will be our main focus in what follows, unless noted otherwise.

1.3 God vs. Abstract Objects

So, from what has been said so far, we have, on the one hand, the concept of the concrete God as the aspatial, eternal, necessary, and first cause and fundamental ground of all things distinct from hirself and, on the other hand, the concept of aspatial, eternal, and necessarily existing abstract objects. If these two concepts of God and abstract objects (respectively) have a nonempty extension, we face what seems to be at least three different problems (sections 1.3.1–1.3.3). I will suggest that we should focus on a more fundamental fourth problem (section 1.3.4).

1.3.1 The Causal Problem

By our concept of God, God is the first cause and creator of all things distinct from hirself. So, if there are abstract objects distinct from God, God is the cause of them, by having created them. But, by our concept of abstract objects, abstract objects are causally inapt and hence cannot be caused by anything,

---

[3] It does not help to think of it as a publicly available concrete inscription of some sort, because two distinct such inscriptions can express one and the same proposition, which raises the same problem all over again.

[4] It is perhaps worth noting that in virtue of grasping an abstract proposition I might do something I otherwise would not have done but it is then still not the abstract proposition as such that enters into the causal chain, only (the concrete) me in virtue of having grasped that abstract proposition.

not even by God's creation. So, the abstract objects are both caused and not caused, which is a direct contradiction. Hence, at least one of our concepts must be wrong, i.e. either empty or in need of modification (see Peter van Inwagen, 2009, 2015, who is pushing a version of this problem).

1.3.2 The Sovereignty Problem

By our concept of God, everything distinct from God is created by God and is under God's creative control. But, if there are causally inapt, eternal, and necessarily existing abstract objects, their being and existence cannot be under God's creative control, since they never were nor could have been different in any way. But then we have a contradiction in the sense that some abstract objects are both under God's creative control and not under God's creative control. Hence, at least one of our concepts must be wrong, i.e. either empty or in need of modification (see Alvin Plantinga, 1980, who is pushing a version of this problem).

1.3.3 The Creation Ex Nihilo Problem

By our concept of God, God is the source in the sense of the creator of *all* things distinct from hirself, which means God created it all out of nothing distinct from hirself. By our concept of abstract objects, there are causally inapt, aspatial, and eternal objects, which means they have always been around (aspatially), have never been created, which in turn means that God cannot have created everything out of nothing distinct from hirself. But then we have a contradiction. Hence, at least one of our concepts must be wrong, i.e. either empty or in need of modification (see William Lane Craig, 2012, 2014, 2017, who is pushing a version of this problem).

1.3.4 The Grounding Problem

Arguably, all three problems end up in what I will here call *the grounding problem*. First, consider the causal problem. Why can God not cause abstract objects? There seems to be two main reasons. First, one might think that abstract objects qua abstract precludes participating in a causal chain, i.e. they are by their nature noncaused. Second, one might think that a cause must exist before its effect, so, in order for God to create abstract objects, there must have been a time at which God but not the abstract objects existed; but since abstract objects are eternal, they have always existed, so there has never been such a time at which God but not the abstract objects existed.

You might find both reasons unconvincing. The main problem is that they both rest on a commonsensical but outdated "billiard ball"–notion of physical causation, where one physical thing causes another physical thing to move due to coming into physical contact with it, where, in addition, the cause must come before the effect in time. But, of course, not only does the world most likely not work like that at a more fundamental level but certainly God of all things need not create things in that way. God, being *God*, can certainly cause something in the sense of create something concrete or abstract at an instant, even before any past point in time. For example, it is logically possible that necessarily, for any point in time, God created all abstract objects before that point in time. One way for this to happen is if the past is indefinitely extensible in the sense that, for any past point in time, there is a point in time before that. From such indefinite extensibility it follows that there has not possibly ever been a point in time at which there were no abstract objects; i.e. abstract objects are necessary and eternal in the sense of always having existed in all possible worlds. One might also take this a step further and postulate a limit-point to the past and say that, necessarily, God simply created everything at that very first instant, which is before any past point in time.

What is more, there is nothing in the concept of an abstract object that entails that such abstract objects qua abstract cannot be created in any sense of the term "create." As we have seen, there is a concept of being created and hence caused at an instant and abstract objects can be caused in that sense of the term. What the concept of abstract objects does preclude is that such objects are caused in some commonsensical "billiard ball"–notion of causation in terms of physical contact; but there is no reason to think such a naïve notion of causation occurs at the fundamental level anyways, and certainly not something God needs to obey. Our concept of abstract objects also seems to preclude that abstract objects cause something concrete (and certainly something physical) but that is neither here nor there; the causal problem is the problem of how something concrete can cause something abstract, not how something abstract can cause something concrete (and certainly not something physical).

So, one here slightly modifies the notion of abstract objects. Instead of saying they are causally inapt, one only says they are more or less ordinarily, or physically, causally inapt.

In short, it is a perfectly coherent position to hold that God is the cause in the sense of creator (at an instant) of all abstract objects but still that both God and abstract objects are necessary, aspatial, and eternal. But the question then is what more exactly is meant by being the creator of something at an instant? As far as I can tell, it is best to think of it as being the *ground* of it. God causing abstract objects at the very first instant, so to speak, then means that God is the ground of their existence at that instant. While commonsensical causation is usually thought of as a *diachronic* relation (across time), grounding is usually thought of as a *synchronic* relation (at a time). The above concept of instant creation before any past point in time is thus best thought of as where the concept of causation and ground meet. In such a picture, God creates in the sense of grounds the abstract realm before any past point in time. But then the question becomes what more exactly is meant by being the ground of abstract objects before any past point in time? That is what I call the *grounding problem*. The causal problem thus arguably ends up in the grounding problem; or perhaps I should instead say that the deeper problem here is the grounding problem. If we solve the grounding problem, we solve the problem of God and abstract objects but, if we only solve the causal problem, we do not thereby solve the problem of God and abstract objects.

Second, consider the sovereignty problem. Why are abstract objects thought to be outside of God's creative control? Presumably because they are necessary, aspatial, and eternal, so they never could have been different in any possible world; they are thus simply not up to God to control. But, by the above concept of instantaneous creation and hence ground of abstract objects before any point in time, there is conceptual room to hold that even though the abstract objects are necessary, aspatial, and eternal, they are still under God's creative control in the sense of God's creative control of what to ground. For example, one might argue that the sense in which the abstract objects must exist is the sense in which they are God's created prerequisite for our concrete existence (cf. Morris & Mentzel, 1986). So, even if God cannot annihilate the abstract without annihilating the concrete, the abstract is still under God's creative control in the sense of being under hir control of what to ground at the instantaneous creation before any past point in time. Also, God (being *God*) can perform so-called *supertasks*. To perform a supertask is to perform a countable infinity of operations in a finite stretch of time. For example, God can count to infinity in one minute. First, God spends 30 seconds counting to 1; then 15 seconds counting to 2; 7.5 seconds counting to 3; 3.25 seconds counting to 4; and so on. Within a minute, God will have reached infinity. God can likewise perform so-called *hypertasks*, which means performing an uncountable infinity of operations, as well as *ultratasks*, which means performing one operation per each ordinal number; all in a finite stretch of time. The notion of a supertask (and hypertask and ultratask) can help make sense of how God can ground or create the entire abstract realm at an instant, but it still being all up to God. We can think of a supertask (or a hypertask or ultratask) but shrink the finite stretch of time arbitrarily close to a point in time. Assuming the task is a free performance by God, we are then in effect considering a free creation and grounding at an instant. There is thus no point in time at which God existed without the abstract realm God also created.

But the question still remains: What more exactly is meant by being the *creator* or *ground* of abstract objects at an instant? We are again facing what I called the grounding problem. In my mind, given the concept of creation at an instant, the sovereignty problem thus also ends up in the grounding problem; or perhaps I should instead say that the deeper problem here is again the grounding problem. By solving the grounding problem, we solve the problem of God and abstract objects but not so by merely solving the sovereignty problem.

Third, consider the creation ex nihilo problem. Why exactly do abstract objects create a problem for creation ex nihilo? Well, because being necessary and eternal, they seem to necessarily always have been around (aspatially), so God cannot have created anything from nothing distinct from hirself, i.e. there were abstract objects around. But there are at least two problems here. First, there are two ways to understand what it means to create something out of nothing. On the one hand, it might mean that initially there is nothing and then you create something. On the other hand, it might mean that initially there might be something and then you create something else but in your creation of that something you use nothing of what else there might have been initially. In both cases, you have created something out of nothing. The creation ex nihilo problem assumes God's creation ex nihilo is of the former sort but it is not obvious that this is the right assumption. Second, even assuming the former sort of creation ex nihilo, in the above picture of creation of all abstract objects at an instant before any past point in time, one might hold that God *did* create and thus ground it all from nothing but *at an instant*. But, still, the question remains: What more exactly is meant by being the creator in the sense of the ground of abstract objects at an infinite past instant? We are again facing what I called the grounding problem; or perhaps I should instead say that, again, the deeper problem here is the grounding problem. Only by solving the grounding problem do we really solve the problem of God and abstract objects.

I thus think the different ways van Inwagen (2009, 2015), Craig (2012, 2017), and (partly) Plantinga (1980) construe the problem of God and abstract objects rest on some unclarities and do not really get to the heart of the matter. Arguably, given the above concept of creation at an instant, the causal problem, the sovereignty problem, and the creation ex nihilo problem all end up in, or should be replaced by, the grounding problem. The question then comes down to this: What does it mean to say that God is the ground of all necessary, aspatial, and eternal abstract objects? We thus do not so much have a contradiction as we have a request for a better understanding of the coexistence of God and abstract objects.

2 The Positions

As we have seen, there are problems with understanding the coexistence of both God and abstract objects. I suggested it is best understood as a problem of how to understand God as the synchronic ground of abstract objects. But, independent of how to best understand the problem, there are in general four kinds of solutions to the problem. One might deny the existence of both God and abstract objects (section 2.1); deny the existence of God but not abstract objects (section 2.2); deny the existence of abstract objects but not God (section 2.3); or accept the existence of both God and abstract objects but try to solve the problem (section 2.4–2.6).

In a sense, the first three kinds of positions avoid the problem by dissolving it, while the last kind tries to solve it more head on. So, though it is worth taking a brief look at the first three kinds of positions as well, note that only the last kind tries to directly answer the problem of the coexistence of God and abstract objects and in particular what I called the grounding problem. We will be mostly interested in the last kind of solution.

2.1 Atheistic Nominalism

According to *Atheism*, there is no God; according to *Nominalism*, there are no abstract objects; so, according to what we should call *Atheistic Nominalism*, there is no God and no abstract objects. Of course, if there is no God and there are no abstract objects, there is no problem with how there can be both such things: there is neither such thing!

For an atheistic nominalist, then, a book on the problem of God and abstract objects holds minimal interest. But there is one way in which the problem might still be of some interest. Assume one is initially agnostic about the existence of one or both of God and abstract objects. Perhaps one finds them both impossible to believe in but equally hard to neglect. On recognizing the deep problem of reconciling God and abstract objects, one might then become convinced of atheistic nominalism as a result.

So an argument could be something like this: it is impossible for both God and abstract objects to exist; neither one's existence is more plausible than the other's; so neither God nor abstract objects exist.

2.2 Atheistic Platonism

According to *Atheism*, there is no God; according to *Platonism*, there are abstract objects; so, according to what we should call *Atheistic Platonism*, there is no God but there are abstract objects. Of course, if there is no God but there are abstract objects, there is no problem with how there can be both such things: there are only abstract objects!

For an atheistic platonist, then, a book on the problem of God and abstract objects holds less interest. But, as with the atheistic nominalist, there is one way in which the problem might still be of some interest. Assume one is initially agnostic about the existence of God, but a firm believer in abstract objects. Perhaps there is nothing in the world one is more convinced of than the truths of the mathematical realm, and though one finds God hard to believe in, God is equally hard to neglect, just think about the fine-tuning argument. But upon recognizing the deep problem of reconciling God and abstract objects, one might then become convinced of Atheistic Platonism as a result.

So, an argument could be something like this: It is impossible for both God and abstract objects to exist; but the existence of abstract objects is undeniable; so, God does not exist.

2.3 Theistic Nominalism

According to *Theism*, God exists; according to *Nominalism*, there are no abstract objects; so, according to what we should call *Theistic Nominalism*, God exists but no abstract objects exist. Of course, if God exists but no abstract objects exist, there is no problem with how there can be both such things: there are no abstract objects!

For a theistic nominalist, then, just like for an atheistic platonist, a book on the problem of God and abstract objects should be of less interest. But, as with the atheistic platonist, there is one way in which the problem might still be of some interest. Assume one is initially agnostic about the existence of abstract objects but a firm believer in God. Perhaps there is nothing in the world one is more convinced of than the existence of God and, though one finds abstract objects hard to believe in, they are equally hard to neglect, just think about the truths of mathematics. But on recognizing the deep problem of reconciling God and abstract objects, one might then become convinced of theistic nominalism as a result.

So, an argument could be something like this: It is impossible for both God and abstract objects to exist; but the existence of God is undeniable; so, abstract objects do not exist.

In fact, this seems to be the line of thought defended by William Lane Craig (2012, 2014, 2017). I do not know if he thinks the existence of God is undeniable but he does fall down in favor of God over abstract objects when confronting the problem of God and abstract objects. More precisely, Craig argues that we can understand all talk about abstract objects in some way that does not involve the real existence of abstract objects and thus can retain our belief in the existence of God over abstract objects. (It is interesting that there seems to be no atheistic platonist out there who argues in the same way, i.e. who argues that we can understand all talk of God in some way that does not involve the real existence of God and thus can retain our belief in abstract objects.)

Recall that, for Craig, the problem of God and abstract objects is first and foremost a problem for God creating ex nihilo (see section 1.3.3), so it makes sense from his perspective to deny the fundamental existence of abstract objects in response to it. Craig therefore naturally chases ways to understand talk of abstract objects that does not involve their real existence. For Plantinga, on the other hand, the problem of God and abstract objects is first and foremost a problem for God's omnipotence and sovereignty (see section 1.3.2), so it makes sense from his perspective to hold that nominalism is neither here nor there (as he indeed argues). For even a theistic nominalist (who is not also a radical modal deflationist) must accept some necessary truths, e.g. theistic nominalism, or Modus Ponens, or that, for any x, x = x; even though there are no abstract objects, it just is not up to God to make such necessary claims false.

So, as always, how we construe the problem matters to what solutions we come to. I have construed the problem in terms of the grounding problem. One of the theistic platonist positions we will discuss in section 2.4.4, namely divine priority, according to which God grounds abstract objects, then becomes a form of theistic nominalism in the sense that, though there are abstract objects in the sense that God grounds them, *most fundamentally* there are no abstract objects. Any position according to which there are abstract objects, but not most fundamentally, we might call *priority nominalism*. Priority nominalism has one advantage over more ordinary nominalism: It need not, as Craig does, chase ways of understanding talk of abstract objects that do not commit to there really being abstract objects. Because, according to priority nominalism, there are abstract objects; they just are not fundamental.

2.4 Theistic Platonism

According to *Theism*, God exists; according to *Platonism*, there are abstract objects; so, according to what we should call *Theistic Platonism*, both God and abstract objects exist. Of course, if both God and abstract objects exist, then we stand face to face with our earlier problems of how there can be both such things. I suggested that, due to the possibility of instant creation before any past point in time, it is best understood in terms of the grounding problem, namely how to understand the grounding relation between God and abstract objects (synchronically, or at a point in time, not diachronically, or across points in time). The grounding problem will be our main focus for the rest of this Element.

As we will soon enough see, grounding is a relation of metaphysical priority. When something is grounded in something else, it is metaphysically explained in terms of that something else, in the sense that the very being of it is what it is in virtue of that something else. Before we look into more details of such a grounding relation, note that there are in general four different positions one could take on such a grounding relationship between God and abstract objects: no priority (section 2.4.1); mutual priority (section 2.4.2); the abstract is prior (section 2.4.3); and God is prior (section 2.4.4). Let us just briefly consider the first three positions before we look into the fourth and most important kind of position in more detail, including some more details of the very notion of grounding in play.

2.4.1 Theistic Platonism: No Priority

According to our concepts of God and abstract objects, they all exist eternally, aspatially, and necessarily. According to one flat-footed position, there is no relation of grounding between God and abstract objects. They all exist eternally, aspatially, and necessarily, independently of each other.

The main problem with this position is that it contradicts both the idea of God as the source of *all* things distinct from hirself and (one of the versions of) the idea of creation ex nihilo. Peter van Inwagen (2009, 2015) seems to think this is no problem at all. In many universally generalized claims, our quantifiers are usually tacitly restricted, e.g. the claim 'There is no beer left!' does not usually entail that there is no beer left in the entire universe, only, for example, that there is no beer left in the fridge (or, in worst-case scenario, in the store). According to him, in the claim that God is the source of all things distinct from hirself, the quantifier "all" is likewise tacitly restricted to all concrete things. According to van Inwagen, just like being omnipotent does not entail that God can make true contradictions (or do anything logically contradictory), so being the source of all things distinct from hirself, and creating it all from nothing, does not entail being the source of abstract objects.

Also, according to van Inwagen (2009), abstract objects are inapt for creation, so, if both God and abstract objects exist, we must simply learn to live with both, with abstract objects being in no way up to God (for a reply to van Inwagen, see Gould, 2014a).

There is no doubt that God, in this picture, is less powerful and foundational than in a picture according to which God is also the source of all abstract objects (if not also of all logical necessities), all being under God's creative control. This solution to the problem thus no doubt amounts to modifying our initial concept of God rather than that of abstract objects, by making God less powerful and foundational. There is also no doubt in my mind that a restriction to concrete objects is an arbitrary and somewhat ad hoc restriction on the quantifier "all" in the claim that God is the source of all things distinct from himself. Why are all and only abstract objects exempted?

Can we do better in the sense of less arbitrariness and less modification to our initial concepts? This is where the notion of grounding comes in.

2.4.2 Theistic Platonism: Mutual Priority

According to our concepts of God and abstract objects, they all exist eternally, aspatially, and necessarily. According to the position we will discuss in this section, there is a mutual (symmetric) priority relation of grounding between them. They all are what they are eternally, aspatially, and necessarily in virtue of each other.

In the earlier case where there is no priority between them, one of them could, *per impossible*, have been what it is without the other. Though it is hard to thus reason with impossible counterfactuals, this does seem to make God less powerful and foundational. Certainly, in that picture, abstract objects are not up to God. But, in the present case where there is mutual grounding between them, none of them can, even *per impossible*, be what it is without the other. If two things are grounded in each other, they are what they are in virtue of each other and hence none of them can be what it is without the other. Though it is again hard to thus reason with impossible counterfactuals, this seems to make room for God being more powerful and foundational than in the no priority view in the previous section.

In the picture we are considering in this section, grounding is symmetric. God and abstract objects are what they are in virtue of each other; none of them being prior to the other. As we will see in section 2.4.4.3, grounding is usually taken to be asymmetric; some might find that to be an objection to the picture we are considering in this section. But why think grounding *must* be asymmetric? Barnes (2018) gives a bunch of cases of plausible symmetric dependence relations. For example, it is plausible to think that, for some objects and properties, those objects and properties depend on each other. One might think with Aristotle that properties cannot exist without objects instantiating them but also that objects cannot exist without instantiating some properties. So, for example, the property of being human cannot exist without humans and humans cannot exist without the property of being human. Symmetric dependence! We are what we are (partly) in virtue of the property of being human and the property of being human is what it is in virtue of us being what we are. Another example might be a fact and its constituents. The fact that I am human is what it is in virtue of me and my humanity and I and my humanity are what we are (partly) in virtue of the fact that I am human.

Can something similar be said of God and abstract objects? Can God and abstract objects be what they are in virtue of each other? One might think that God has a *nature*, i.e. some essential properties without which God would not be God. One might further think that God and God's nature are grounded in or are what they are in virtue of each other. That might in effect be a mutual (symmetric) grounding between God and *some* abstract objects but can there be such a mutual grounding between God and *all* necessary, aspatial, and eternal abstract objects? Plantinga (1980, pp. 140–146) suggests that maybe part of what it is to be God is to affirm *all* necessary abstract objects and corresponding truths and that all those abstract objects and truths are what they are in virtue of God affirming them. That would in effect be a picture in which God and abstract objects are mutually dependent on each other.

But such a picture is violating the thesis of DF, so, to the extent one holds on to DF, one must let go of such a picture of mutual dependence. As Plantinga (1980, pp. 145–146) also suggests, it would indeed be nice if there was a way to go further and understand how God can also, somehow, be prior to all those abstract objects, i.e. how God can in addition to eternally and necessarily affirming them also ground them. Such a position is what we will discuss under the heading of *divine priority* in section 2.4.4 but, first, we should take a quick look at the opposite view, according to which abstract objects are prior to God.

2.4.3 Theistic Platonism: Abstract Priority

According to our concepts of God and abstract objects, they all exist eternally, aspatially, and necessarily. According to the position we are interested in here, the abstract realm grounds God in the sense that God's being holds in virtue of the abstract realm (and not vice versa).

Obviously, abstract objects have not created God at an instant, since abstract objects do not do anything whatsoever, so the priority of abstract objects over God must be a mere grounding relation in some sense of noncreation. Neither God nor abstract objects could have failed to exist but God is nonetheless grounded in the abstract objects. The abstract objects are thus more fundamental than God. Though, according to this position, God exists, there is a sense in which it becomes a form of what we might call *priority atheism*: most fundamentally, there is no God, only abstract objects; God is derivative of them. This position thus not only denies both DF and creation ex nihilo but also lays down obvious restrictions on God's aseity and sovereignty. As a theistic position, it is thus of less interest, I think. Proponents of this position are Pythagoreans, who should worship the empty set instead of God.

2.4.4 Theistic Platonism: Divine Priority

According to our concepts of God and abstract objects, they all exist eternally, aspatially, and necessarily. According to the kind of position we'll discuss in this section, the abstract realm is grounded in God, like all other things distinct from God. This position is thus the position that most respects DF, as well as God's aseity and sovereignty. With the concept of creation at an instant on board, it can also respect God's creation ex nihilo. The position comes in several different versions, each with its own distinctive pros and cons. We will consider two main versions of it, absolute creationism (section 2.4.4.1) and divine conceptualism (section 2.4.4.2), before we look at the notion of grounding involved in more detail to see whether that helps (section 2.4.4.3).

2.4.4.1 Divine Priority: Absolute Creationism

According to *absolute creationism* (AC), God created all objects, including all abstract objects, and it is up to God to change, or even annihilate, them. Since propositions are abstract objects, it follows from this position that God could have made true propositions impossible and impossible propositions true. So, God could have made it the case that the empty set did not exist or that no mathematical objects existed; God could also have made it the case that nothing is self-identical, i.e. that everything is non–self-identical. When God made it necessarily so that the empty set exists, or any other mathematical object, and that everything is self-identical, it was a choice God made; God could have made a different choice about these matters. All necessary and impossible existences and truths are contingent on God's free creation.

A version of AC is defended by René Descartes (1630), according to whom God could have made all of mathematics false. Descartes' view is often called *universal possibilism*. More recently, Brian Leftow (2012) defends something similar, according to whom *it is in God* to have made different abstract objects, or no abstract objects. But, as we will see in the next section, Leftow's view is a reductionistic view, where the abstract objects are really, most fundamentally, concrete parts of God's mind. AC on the other hand, need not be reductionistic. According to AC, abstract objects might be as real as concrete objects, both being equally created by God and being equally up to God to change, or even annihilate.

A flat-footed objection to AC is that God could then have made hirself an impossible existent, and all deductive argumentation invalid, as well as everything non–self-identical, which makes everything straightforwardly incoherent, making all talk and thought about anything impossible, at least for us humans. But we can be more charitable, because there are ways of making better sense of AC, at least avoiding making it straightforwardly incoherent.

The idea is to insist that God created all things, including all abstract objects, but that we cannot say much about what God could have done differently with respect to them. We can start with a *primitive* operator, G, operating on propositions (which we express through sentences). We say that Gp is true if and only if God grounds that p (i.e. that p is true). We then introduce a *modal* operator, P, which also operates on propositions. We say that Pp is true if and only if it is possible that p, and that it is possible that p if and only if God grounds that possibly p; so Pp is true if and only if $G(P$p).[5] We then define another modal operator, N, also operating on propositions. We say that Np is true if and only if it is not the case that it is possible that *not-P*, i.e. if and only if it is necessary that p. Finally, we stipulate that P and N can never occur outside of the scope (i.e. to the left) of G in a sentence; any such sentence with P or N outside of G is taken to be literally senseless. Now, in this language, we can meaningfully say things of the form Pp, Np, Gp, and even $G(P$p) and $G(N$p) but nothing of the form $P(G$p) or $N(G$p); the latter makes no sense in this picture.

Now, with such a restriction on the operators, we can say that $G(N$(everything is self-identical)) but not that $P(G$(something is non–self-identical)) or $G(P(G$(something is non–self-identical))). The latter makes no sense in this picture. Likewise, we can say that $G(N$(there is an empty set)) and we can say that $G($*not-P*(there is no empty set)) but we cannot say, for example, that it is possible that God made no empty set. In order to say so, we would have to (*per impossibile*) say either that $P(G$(there is no empty set)) or that $G(P(G$(there is no empty set))) but then, in either case, P occurs outside (to the left) of G, which is precisely what is forbidden in this picture.

The best way to think of it is perhaps by noting that since God created all abstract objects, including all of modal space, he also created the ways we can and cannot talk, think, and make sense of things; we thus just cannot make sense of things outside of our modal space, i.e. outside the scope of G. It is sort of like a camera that is made to take pictures of many things but not of itself. To paraphrase early Wittgenstein, what we cannot talk about we must, unfortunately, pass over in silence.

The problem is that this is not really full-blown AC but a slightly restricted version of it, which we might call *quietist AC*, where we are not explicitly saying that God could have made necessary existents and truths nonexistent and false; it is just that we are also not saying that he could not do so.

---

[5] Obviously, we are not here taking this to be a reductive explanation of possibility.

Morris and Menzel (1986) defend a view similar to AC. I say similar because it is ambiguous what exactly their view is. On the one hand, they say that "our suggestion is that the platonistic framework of reality arises out of a creatively efficacious intellective activity of God … an intellectual activity of God's is responsible for the [platonistic] framework of reality" (p. 356). This suggests that the platonistic framework (i.e. all abstract objects) is up to God to change or even annihilate, which suggests AC. But they also say that "there is no Archimedean point outside the actual conceiving activity of God from which we could judge it to be possible that God conceive a framework different from the one which in fact, and of necessity, gives us all possibility and all necessity" (p. 357). This suggests that we cannot really think and talk about alternative abstract objects, which suggests something like the quietist AC above. But, on the other hand, they say that these abstract objects are "God's concepts, the products, or perhaps better, the *contents* of a divine intellective activity … [but they are] not ontologically independent, but rather depend on certain divine activities" (p. 355) They go on to say that

> the necessity of his creating the framework is not imposed on him from without, but rather is a feature and result of the nature of his own activity itself, which is a function of what he is … If we are right, theists can acknowledge the standard platonist view that God is not in control of abstract objects or necessary truths, in the sense that he cannot annihilate or alter them intrinsically, while at the same time maintaining that these things depend on God for their existence and intrinsic characteristics. (p. 357)

This straightforwardly suggests that it is *not* up to God to change or annihilate abstract objects. So, are the abstract objects all up to God or not?

What makes it even more confusing is that the title of their paper is "Absolute creation" but they call the view they defend in the paper "theistic activism," which is supposed to preserve the virtues but avoid the vices of Descartes' notorious *universal possibilism* mentioned in section 2.4.4.1. Their view does not seem to be AC, if by that term we mean absolute by "absolute," nor universal possibilism, if by that term we mean universal by "universal." A question that arises is therefore: What is the active element in their theistic activism?

Craig (2017, pp. 121–129) is also puzzled by what more exactly the view Morris and Menzel defend amounts to. For Craig, the ambiguity seems to first and foremost be between AC and the view we will discuss in the next section, namely *divine conceptualism*, according to which abstract objects are identical with parts of God's mental life. Craig falls down on the better interpretation of their view being AC over divine conceptualism. I agree, but I think an even better interpretation of Morris and Menzel is that their view is an attempt at answering a question raised by Plantinga (1980, pp. 145–146), namely whether God's mental activity can be metaphysically *prior to* the necessary existence of abstract objects, even though God cannot change or annihilate them? In other words, is there a sense in which abstract objects are *grounded in* God's mental activity even though God cannot change or annihilate them? Morris and Menzel's answer is: yes. God is the absolute creator of all abstract objects and, in some sense or other, they all thus depend on God's mind, or God's mind is prior to them all, but nonetheless God cannot change or annihilate them. Even though they are grounded in God's mind, abstract objects are not identical with parts of God's mind; abstract objects are necessarily and always what they are.

Davison (1991) criticizes their view for not really going into any details as to what such terms as "in virtue of" and "grounded" might mean here. Morris and Menzel use terms such as "responsible for," "a result of," and "dependence," and even switch to "causal dependence," but do not say much as to what they mean more exactly. They claim to distinguish "carefully between issues of dependence and control" (Morris & Menzel, 1986, p. 358) but it remains a mere claim without any further clarification of neither "dependence" nor "control." True, they separate logical dependence from causal dependence, by claiming that, though God and abstract objects are logically dependent on each other by the fact that both are necessary existents, abstract objects are (nontemporally) causally dependent on God but God is not in any sense causally dependent on abstract objects. But that is more pointing to the problem than solving it. The problem remains how more exactly abstract objects can be causally dependent on God.

I take it this last is the grounding problem we ended up with in section 1. This is also the problem we will look into in more detail in section 2.4.4.3. But, first, it is worth looking at an interesting problem for AC and also for Morris and Menzel's position, namely the so-called *bootstrapping problem*. This will help us better see what is at stake here.

If God is supposed to be a personal being worthy of worship, then, pace the thesis of divine simplicity, it is plausible that God also has a *nature*, a collection of *essential* properties without which God would not be God. But, presumably, God is not identical to a mere collection of properties, so God is not identical with hir nature. Rather, God instantiates hir nature. But then the question becomes: Who, or what, created God's nature? If God is not identical with hir nature, but is supposed to be the source of all things distinct from hirself, then God must be the source of hir own nature. But that seems impossible because God cannot be God without hir nature, so God cannot be the source of hir nature because that source, prior to the nature in question, would not be God. This is what I will here mean by the so-called bootstrapping problem.

Morris and Menzel provide an interesting picture that tries to make sense of how God *can* be the source of hir own nature after all. They envision what they call the *materialization machine*, which we might very well today think of as a 3D printer that can print its own parts. Just think of a 3D printer that can print pretty much anything, call it 3DP. After having run for a while, one of 3DP's parts is starting to wear out. So, 3DP prints out that part, which is then replaced with the old part before it breaks down. After a while, all of 3DP's parts have been replaced. So far, so good. Now, simply imagine further that 3DP has no initial source for its existence. 3DP has necessarily and always been around, printing things, including its own parts before they wear out. There is then a natural sense in which 3DP is the source of all of its own parts; 3DP is (nontemporally) prior to its parts. That is, the parts of 3DP and 3DP are logically dependent on each other in the sense that they both necessarily and always exist, but the parts of 3DP are nonetheless grounded in 3DP in a way that 3DP is not grounded in its parts.

Morris and Menzel claim that God's nature might be similarly grounded in God in a way that God is not grounded in God's nature, showing that the idea of God being the source in the sense of ground of hir own nature is not an incoherent idea, which dissolves the bootstrapping problem in the sense that there is no problem here after all. Note that, in this picture, even though God grounds hir own nature, God does not ground hirself. God thus remains the ground of all things distinct from hirself, including all abstract objects, which includes hir own nature; God hirself remains ungrounded.

I find this analogy of God and 3DP very interesting. It helps elucidate how God can ground all abstract objects, including hir own nature, even though they all are necessary, aspatial, and eternal things. It also helps us better see all that is at stake. It is not just a matter of explaining how God can ground abstract objects but also how God can ground hir own nature, unless we are to try to accept the thesis of divine simplicity, i.e. that God is a mereologically atomic structureless thing (for an interesting such attempt, see Fowler, 2015).

Craig (2017, pp. 140–144) objects that Morris and Menzel's picture of the materialization machine, our 3DP, solves for the wrong kind of circularity. According to Craig, "Morris and Menzel want to show, in effect, that while God causes His properties, His properties do not cause God" (p. 142). But, according to Craig, relying on Bergmann and Brower (2006), the circularity consists instead in God needing some property or other in order to create properties. But I think Craig is here implicitly working with a notion of diachronic causation, while Morris and Menzel are working with a notion of synchronic causation, closer to what I have called grounding. Of course, God needs to have some properties before he can create properties, if we think of it diachronically, but what 3DP shows is that there is also a coherent notion according to which God can ground all properties, including hir own nature, if we think of it synchronically. And, according to Plantinga (1980), Morris and Menzel (1986), and me (section 1), the problem is ultimately a problem of synchronic creation, or instantaneous creation before any past point in time, not diachronic creation. The question is how God can ground abstract objects given that they are all necessary, aspatial, and eternal, not how God can diachronically cause them.

Another way of putting this is that the bootstrapping problem comes in two different versions, a diachronic version and a synchronic version. In section 1, we saw how the causal problem, the creation ex nihilo problem, and the sovereignty problem are all problems that arguably end up in what I called the grounding problem. Craig (2017) construes the problem of God and abstract objects as, first and foremost, the creation ex nihilo problem and he thinks of creation as a more or less diachronic causal matter. So, naturally, while Craig is concerned with the diachronic version of the bootstrapping problem, in this Element, we are (and I believe Plantinga and Morris and Menzel are as well) more concerned with the synchronic version of the bootstrapping problem.

But another problem remains. Even if it is coherent to hold the view that God can be the ground of all abstract objects, including hir own nature, it is not obvious that we would thereby have an answer to the question whether it is up to God to change or annihilate the abstract objects. As we saw earlier in this section, Morris and Menzel (1986) claim that "the necessity of his creating the framework is not imposed on him from without, but rather is a feature and result of the nature of his own activity itself, which is a function of what he is" (p. 357). They go on to explicitly say that "if we are right, theists can acknowledge the standard platonist view that God is not in control of abstract objects or necessary truths, in the sense that he cannot annihilate or alter them intrinsically, while at the same time maintaining that these things depend on God for their existence and intrinsic characteristics" (p. 357). This seems to indicate that they operate with a notion of creation that is not necessarily a fully free creation but rather one that is restrained by what God is, i.e. by God's nature. The creation of abstract objects is thus restricted by and dependent on God's nature.

Craig (2017, pp. 134–135) objects that this restricts God's freedom of creation. But does it? In the picture sketched above, God's nature is grounded in God, so, by transitivity of grounding, whatever is grounded in God's nature is grounded in God. Now, God's creation of abstract objects is grounded in God's nature and God's nature is grounded in God, so God's creation of abstract objects is thereby grounded in God. Should, or can, we even ask for more freedom in creation than that? Being free does not mean being under no constraints whatsoever. What would such a notion of freedom even mean? Being under no possible constraints, not even under the constraints of reason, seems being no more free than being under all possible constraints. Freedom has to be somewhere in the middle of these two extremes. Freedom is about being able to choose between different options but not between all logically possible options at the same time without any constraints whatsoever.

Craig might thus be asking for an impossible kind of freedom. Admittedly, this is a very complex issue, an issue we cannot dig into here, but recall that Morris and Menzel (1986) also claim that "there is no Archimedean point outside the actual conceiving activity of God from which we could judge it to be possible that God conceive a framework different from the one which in fact, and of necessity, gives us all possibility and all necessity" (p. 357). In response to Craig, they might thus not only be understood as grounding abstract objects in God but also be proposing a version of what we earlier called quietist AC; and, likewise, in the end, might all proponents of AC. To paraphrase early Wittgenstein again, what we cannot talk about we must, unfortunately, pass over in silence. Unfortunately, the deeper true notion of freedom might lie hidden somewhere in this necessary silence.

Let us close this section by noting that AC and quietist AC are neutral on whether abstract objects are distinct from God's mind. All AC is claiming is that abstract objects are up to God to create, change, and destroy and all quietist AC is claiming is that abstract objects are up to God to create. That says nothing as to whether they are parts of God's mind. The thesis that they are parts of God's mind is known as *divine conceptualism*, which we turn to next.

2.4.4.2 Divine Priority: Divine Conceptualism

According to *divine conceptualism* (DC), abstract objects are parts of God's mind (see Leftow, 2012; Welty, 2014). According to one version of it, abstract objects are God's ideas, properties are God's concepts, and propositions are God's thoughts. So, when we think of an abstract object, a property, or grasp a proposition, we think of God's ideas, concepts, or grasp hir thoughts.

The main difference between DC and AC, which we looked at in the previous section, is thus that, while AC claims that all eternal, aspatial, and necessarily existing abstract objects are completely up to God, but makes no claim as to any of it being a part of God's mind, DC claims that abstract objects are parts of God's mind, but makes no claim as to all of its eternal, aspatial, and necessarily existing abstract objects being up to God. So, for example, while AC claims that the existence of the empty set is created and made eternal, aspatial, and necessary by God, and that it is up to God to change it to being temporally finite, spatial, contingent, or impossible, but makes no claim that it is a part of God's mind, DC claims that the empty set is a part of God's mind and that its eternal, aspatial, and necessary existence is made so by God, but makes no claim that it is up to God to change or annihilate it.

By leaving it open whether abstract objects are up to God, DC really comes in two kinds: on the one hand, they are parts of God's mind that it is up to God to change but, on the other hand, they are parts of God's mind that it is not up to God to change. While the former takes us closer to AC, the latter raises anew Craig's objection of restricting God's freedom of creation, which we looked at in the previous section. But, in any case, for present purposes the important feature of DC is that abstract objects are parts of God's mind, so, when we grasp them, we grasp parts of God's mind.

Craig (2017, chap. 5) objects, rightly in my mind, that, by identifying abstract objects with parts of God's mind, DC becomes a form of nominalism. All forms of mental activity are concrete things, not abstract things. That is, although the *content* of a mental activity might be abstract, the mental activity itself is something concrete. So, if abstract objects are to be identified with God's mental activity, they are really concrete things, not abstract things. So, this solution to the problem of God and abstract objects is really a form of the solution we looked at in section 2.3, namely a form of theistic nominalism in the sense that, ultimately, it denies there being any abstract objects.

One might reply that abstract objects are the *contents* of God's mental activity, not the mental activity itself. But the problem is that raises the question of what the relationship between God and hir abstract mental content is. In many ways, it thus simply recreates the problem of God and abstract objects. So, the dilemma is: Either abstract objects are concrete objects (mental events), in which case we have a version of theistic nominalism, or abstract objects are really abstract objects, in which case we are back at the grounding problem. (Leftow [2012] seems to accept the former; Welty [2014] seems to accept the latter.)

Grounding is usually not taken to be identity. So, if abstract objects are grounded in God's mind, we need not, and perhaps should not, take them to be identical to any parts of God's mind. We can thus avoid Craig's objection that divine conceptualism is a kind of theistic nominalism and side with Welty (and I believe Morris and Menzel) in taking them to be genuinely abstract objects but nonetheless grounded in God's mind. In the next section, we will try to understand such a relation of grounding without it being identity. It is in any case high time to look into the notion of grounding itself in some more detail to see whether it might help us solve the grounding problem with respect to God and abstract objects.

2.4.4.3 Divine Priority: Hyperintensional Grounding

The grounding problem is how God can create everything at an instant in the sense of how necessary, aspatial, and eternal abstract objects can be synchronically grounded in God. So far, we have been very casual in our mention and use of the notion of grounding involved in that problem. Unfortunately, digging into the details of grounding is of limited help for our purposes. In this final subsection of section 2, I will try to show why.

Over the last decade or two, much due to Fine (2001), Schaffer (2009), and Rosen (2010), there has been an enormous growth in philosophical work on the notion of grounding. As always in philosophy, there is not much agreement on what exactly the notion of grounding amounts to but the closest we get to a standard notion (see Bliss & Trogdon, 2014; Raven, 2015) is by thinking of grounding as a many-one relation among facts: the (one or more) facts that qq ground the (one) fact that p. For example, the facts behind the atoms being arranged tablewise ground the fact that there is a table. That is, the fact that the table is there holds in virtue of the facts behind the atoms being arranged tablewise. Such a relation of grounding is usually taken to be a *strict partial ordering*, meaning it has three formal properties. First, it is *irreflexive*: no fact that p grounds itself. Second, it is *asymmetric*: if the facts that qq ground p, then no facts rr are such that they together with p ground any one of qq. Third, it is *transitive*: if the facts qq ground the fact that p, and the facts rr and p ground the fact that s, then qq and rr ground the fact that s. So, for example, the fact that there is a table does not ground itself; if the facts behind the atoms being arranged tablewise ground the fact that there is a table, the fact that there is a table does not even partially ground any of the facts behind the atoms being arranged tablewise; and, roughly, if the facts behind the atoms being arranged tablewise ground the fact that there is a table and the facts behind the subatomic particles being arranged atomwise ground the facts behind the atoms being arranged tablewise, then the facts behind the subatomic particles being arranged atomwise ground the fact that there is a table. By these three formal properties, grounding thus always takes us downwards in the grounding hierarchy.

Grounding is supposed to be a metaphysically explanatory relation, an explanation of what something consists in more fundamentally, which makes it plausible that it is also *nonmonotonic*, meaning that, if the facts that qq ground the fact that p, then we cannot add another arbitrary fact r to the explanation such that qq and r ground the fact that p. If qq ground p, then adding facts to qq ruins the explanation of p. For example, if the facts behind the atoms being arranged tablewise ground the fact that there is a table, then the facts behind the atoms being arranged tablewise together with the fact that I am drinking coffee is a worse, if any, explanation of the fact that there is a table.

The claim that grounding is an explanatory relation is usually taken at face value: the grounding relation itself is the explanation. Such an explanatory grounding relation is also often taken to be *necessitating*: if qq ground p, then necessarily, if qq hold, then p holds. So, for example, if the facts behind the atoms arranged tablewise ground the fact that there is a table, then, in any other possible world, if the facts behind the atoms arranged tablewise are the same there, then there is a table there too. In a sense, the table is not much (if anything) other than what grounds it. In general, the holding of the ground is all it takes for the grounded to hold as well.

Grounding is also often taken to be *well-founded*, meaning that any grounded fact p is ultimately grounded in some *un*grounded facts qq. So, for example, if the facts behind the atoms arranged tablewise ground the fact that there is a table, then the fact that there is a table will ultimately end up being grounded in some most fundamental facts that themselves have no further ground; be they the facts behind the subatomic particles being arranged the way they are or some even more fundamental facts in turn underlying the subatomic particles being arranged the way they are. The general idea is that metaphysical explanation must come to an end, eventually (against this idea, see Bohn, 2018a).

Finally, grounding is taken to be *hyperintensional*: it is a nonmodal relation that can also hold among necessary facts. So, for example, facts about sets are presumably grounded in facts about their members, and hence the being of, e.g., the set of the empty set is presumably grounded in the being of the empty set, even though both the empty set and the set of the empty set must exist. This is an important feature for present purposes. By focusing on grounding as a hyperintensional, nonmodal notion, we avoid all problems with trying to analyze the relationship between God and abstract objects in terms of modal notions of dependence, possible worlds, and/or counterfactuals. Many discussions over such modal notions in, e.g., Morris and Menzel (1986), Davison (1991), and even Craig (2017) are thus obsolete at this point.

Now, can this more or less standard notion of grounding help solve our grounding problem of how necessary, aspatial, and eternal abstract objects are grounded in God? I doubt it. The notion in play certainly cannot be exactly as the more or less standard notion explicated above. If grounding is supposed to relate the nonfundamental to the fundamental, and God is supposed to be the one and only most fundamental thing, then grounding should be able to relate all things distinct from God, objects as well as facts, to *God*, not merely to the *fact* that there is a God. There is a big difference between saying that something is grounded in *the fact that* there is a God and saying that something is grounded in *God*. For present theistic purposes, only being able to say the former is inadequate; a theist wants to be able to say the latter. It is God hirself that is the one and only most fundamental thing, not the mere fact that there is a God. So, for present purposes, grounding should be able to relate all kinds of things, including objects and persons as well as facts. (We must thus look more in the direction of Schaffer's [2009; 2010; 2016b] notion of grounding than in the direction of Fine's [2001] or Rosen's [2010] notion of grounding.)

Grounding should remain a well-founded, strict partial ordering, though, and thus only take us downwards in the metaphysically explanatory hierarchy, ending in God. Everything is ultimately grounded in God, or parts of God, which is not grounded in anything else, nor does God ground hirself. God is *un*grounded. This is as it should be for our theist. Like Tillich (1973) famously points out, God cannot be a thing like any other thing; God must be special, what explains all other things. We can thus see that, in addition to being a strict partial ordering, grounding is, in this picture, also well-founded, as per the more or less standard notion explicated earlier in this section. It is also nonmonotonic: Adding distinct things to God ruins the theistic explanation of God being the one and only ground of all things distinct from God; this includes adding abstract objects to the explanation.

What about the feature of necessitation? If God grounds something, does God necessitate it? If God grounds something, and God necessarily exists (i.e. the thesis of DN is true), then, by necessitation, that something also necessarily exists. But, since God is supposed to ground all things distinct from hirself, then all things distinct from God necessarily exist. This is *Necessitism* (Williamson, 2013), the thesis according to which, necessarily, all things necessarily exist. If such Necessitism is true, the problem is no longer just God and necessarily existing abstract objects but God and any necessarily existing objects, abstract and concrete. Necessarily existing abstract objects become a problem only insofar as they are abstract; the more general problem is now how God can ground *any* necessarily existing things. According to Necessitism, for many things, *what* it is could have been different but *that* it is could not have been different, i.e. its nature is contingent but its existence is necessary. So, if Necessitism is true, though their nature might be, no thing's existence is up to God!

For our theist, it is therefore better to give up the feature of necessitation of grounding. Instead she should claim that God grounds all things distinct from hirself but, at least for many of them, i.e. the contingent concrete things, if not for all the necessary abstract things, God could have chosen not to create them and thus not to ground them. This also sits better with the idea that God *created* everything at an instant. Presumably, this notion of creation is a notion of a free, creative, and productive process, so it should not be a relation of necessitation. The challenge is of course to further explicate how there can be such a free, creative, and productive process at an instance. The more or less standard notion of grounding alone does not seem up to the task.

In what sense should grounding be explanatory? Consider the usual sense in which grounding itself is the explanation. This makes most sense when grounding relates facts, or true propositions, which are the kind of things that can explain each other, but it is hard to make sense of when grounding also relates objects, and other things, as per our theist's notion of grounding. The facts, or true propositions, behind the atoms arranged tablewise can explain the fact or true proposition that there is a table but how can the atoms arranged tablewise themselves explain the table itself? How can objects explain anything? Though it hardly makes sense to say that objects explain other objects, it does make sense to say that a grounding relation among objects is what our (true) metaphysical explanation *tracks*. For example, the grounding of the table in the atoms arranged tablewise is what the explanation of the being of the table is tracking.

So, instead of holding grounding to itself be a metaphysical explanation, our theist should hold grounding to be what a metaphysical explanation tracks (cf. Schaffer, 2016b). So, God grounding all things distinct from hirself does not in itself metaphysically explain all things distinct from God but all things distinct from God being grounded in God is what our (true) metaphysical explanation of them is tracking; just like a (true) causal explanation is tracking causal relations.

Finally, grounding must be hyperintensional because both God and the abstract objects in question are necessarily existing things; what we are asking is precisely whether there is some such hyperintensional notion of grounding.

Now, let us get back to our main question: Can abstract objects be thus grounded in God? For example, can the empty set be grounded in God's essential feature of believing that there is an empty set? The problem is that we can keep saying that abstract objects are thus grounded in God's nature, and even as earlier in this section explicate what we mean by "grounding" in so saying, but it still does not seem to help much toward explaining the being of the empty set. The explanation in terms of grounding by itself is too opaque to be of much help. In the case of a table being grounded in some atoms arranged tablewise, the explanation in terms of grounding has a level of transparency that makes it plausible: The table is nothing but those atoms, so facts about those atoms explain the being of the table! Of course, this transparency rests on our supposed known physical theories about the nature of tables. But, in the case of the empty set being grounded in God's nature, there seems to be no such transparency and hence no such plausibility. We simply lack the additional theory, or just a simple story, that can make the grounding transparent.

So we must try to come up with such additional theories, or stories, making the grounding more transparent. Here is one possible additional such theory for our particular case at hand. One of the axioms of set theory is that there is an empty set, i.e. a set with no members. What makes this axiomatic proposition an eternal and necessary truth (and hence fact)? Well, there is a God who always and necessarily has some thoughts and not others. For example, God always and necessarily has the purely logical thought that for every x, $x = x$; likewise, God always and necessarily has the thought that there is an empty set. Having such thoughts, and not others (e.g. that there is a round square who is red and blue all over at the same time), is part of God's nature, which it is not up to God to change, at least not all at once. So, when we grasp the necessarily true proposition that there is an empty set, we grasp one of God's essential thoughts, which even God cannot stop having. This in turn might help explain the eternal and necessarily existing abstract empty set. When we grasp that there is an empty set, what we are grasping is an eternal and necessary proposition, which is one of God's eternal and necessary thoughts. Any one of God's thoughts is in turn grounded in God in the sense that God having that thought is nothing but a part of God's nature. In the case of God's thoughts of abstract objects, we should further take the whole thought to be more fundamental than the object and property the thought might be carved up into. That is, the object and the property are abstractions from the thought, not the other way around. Finally, that is the sense in which the eternally and necessarily existing empty set is grounded in God: It is an abstraction from one of God's thoughts. So, in sum, the abstract objects are grounded in abstract facts, which in turn are grounded in God's thoughts, which in turn are grounded in God, which is the fundamental ungrounded ground of all things.

With such an additional theory, or story, onboard, the grounding explanation of the empty set in terms of God makes more sense, in a more transparent way; much like the table being grounded in the atoms arranged tablewise. In both cases, we can start to see how it goes. But, to paraphrase Wittgenstein (again), the abstract realm is a realm of divine thoughts, not objects. Most fundamentally, there are no abstract objects, only divine thoughts (from which God and we can in turn abstract objects).

One might object that all thoughts, including the thoughts of God, are essentially intentional and thus must be about something external to the thought. So, God's thought about there being an empty set must be about something external to that thought. But this objection is not convincing. Arguably, thoughts can be intentional without being about something *external* to thought. I can make up and have thoughts about a fictional character and, by abstraction, think and talk about it, without my thoughts thereby being about something external to my own thoughts. My thoughts are merely about the fictional character abstracted from my thoughts. I can then communicate my thought to you. When you in turn think and talk about it, you ultimately think and talk about my thoughts. After a while, we can abstract new thoughts and objects from our collective thoughts. Likewise, God can have thoughts about mathematical objects (or any other abstract objects) and, by abstraction, think and talk about them, and even have us think and talk about them, without any of our thoughts thereby being in the end, most fundamentally, about something not grounded in God's thoughts. Our thoughts are merely about the mathematical objects abstracted from our thoughts. What is more, just like some thoughts are essential to me, e.g. that everything is self-identical, so some thoughts are essential to God, e.g. all true mathematical thoughts.

At least, some such reply must be developed in response to the objection that God's thoughts must be about something external to God's mind. Because, if not, we get the whole problem of God and abstract objects all over again.

I believe the kind of position discussed in this section – Divine Priority: Hyperintensional Grounding – is the most plausible kind of position in response to the grounding problem. The notion of grounding involved needs to be somewhat modified compared to what is perhaps a more standard notion but digging too much into the details of the very notion of grounding does not help solve our problem; rather, we need a complementary story making the grounding explanation more comprehensible, or transparent. The remaining problem is how to best complete that story.

3 Toward a New Position: Divine Informationalism

In sections 1 and 2, we looked at the problem of God and abstract objects and possible solutions to it. We ended up with the position according to which God grounds all abstract objects. But we also saw that all the solutions had problems of their own; in particular, merely saying that abstract objects are grounded in God does not seem to help much to resolve those problems; we need an additional story. Instead of trying to give that story in more detail, in this section, I want to question some of the more implicit presuppositions of the problem.

I will not question the existence of either God or abstract objects but I will question one of the most basic presuppositions for the entire problem to arise in the first place, namely that our fundamental ontology is that of objects and properties. I suggest considering instead it being one of information. It is common to think of objects and properties as basic kinds of entities, from which we can derive information (as well as other kinds of things). But I suggest we instead think of information as a basic kind of thing, from which we can derive objects and properties (as well as other kinds of things). As we will see, in this picture, the problem of God and abstract objects dissolves without having to give up either theism or Platonism. That is an interesting position, worthy of more attention.

First, I consider the nature of information (section 3.1); second, I consider the thesis that, most fundamentally, there is only information (section 3.2); third, I consider the thesis that God is that most fundamental information and discuss how this solves the problem of God and abstract objects (section 3.3); and, fourth, I reconsider the abstract/concrete distinction and consider a new suggestion according to which God is not only the one and only fundamental entity but also the one and only fully concrete entity there is and can be (section 3.4). The idea is that God is the one and only fully informational being.

3.1 Information

What is information? There are at least three distinct kinds of notions in play (cf. Shannon & Weaver, 1949; Dretske, 1981; Floridi, 2011; Dembski, 2014; Adriaans, 2018). First, there is information *about* reality, which we might call *semantic* information. For example, the proposition that I feel I am getting old has a meaning that carries information about reality, namely about me and my feelings about my age. Second, there is information *for* reality, which we might call *algorithmic* information. For example, some laws of nature can be thought of as algorithms of the form: if this happens, then perform that. The difference between information about reality and information for reality is perhaps better seen by considering a law of nature formulated as a proposition. For example, consider the proposition that an object in a vacuum will keep moving in a uniform way until something external to it influences it. This proposition carries information about reality in the sense that it says something about reality but it also carries information for reality in the sense that it "tells" reality how to behave.

Third, and most importantly for our purposes, there is information *as* reality, which we might call *metaphysical* information. For example, one might think of an electron as first and foremost a physical object from which we can extract (semantic) information that we can (algorithmically) process. But one might also think of an electron as first and foremost pure information that can be coded in various ways (concretely or abstractly), (semantically) understood, and (algorithmically) processed. In this latter picture, the concrete and physical aspects of an electron are most fundamentally nothing but the information the electron communicates to us. Of course, an electron is only one example; the same goes for all objects, physical, mental, concrete and abstract. It is this last way of thinking of things that will be our focus in what follows.

A discussion of the exact relationship between semantic, algorithmic, and metaphysical information must be left for another time but note that metaphysical information is to be *identified* with neither semantic nor algorithmic information. Compare this to a sentence. Whatever a sentence is, is to be identified with neither what the sentence is about nor what it "tells" us to do. Whatever meaning we attach to it, and whatever anyone or anything does with it, is different from whatever it is. But, in order to carry meaning, or "tell" us what to do, it must be something. The same goes for information. Information must itself be something in order to carry information or instructions. We are interested in whatever that something is, not whatever meaning or action is attached to it. We are here and henceforth thus ignoring the notions of semantic and algorithmic information, only focusing on the nature of information, unless noted otherwise.

I will now make a radical claim, namely that when we think about it, the nature of metaphysical information is not so obviously less understood than the nature of either concrete or abstract objects. For example, consider physical (and hence concrete) objects. It is well known that it is notoriously hard to define what it is to be physical. For example, it cannot be whatever contemporary physics says it is because it is also well known that contemporary physics is not only incomplete but close to inconsistent. Aspects of relativity theory (behavior of large things) and quantum mechanics (behavior of small things) do not sit well together, so the fully true physics cannot be exactly what it is today. So, if being physical is defined by whatever contemporary physics says, then, most likely, nothing is truly physical. But, if we say it is whatever future physics says it is, then, since no one knows what a complete and consistent future physics will bring, no one knows what it is to be physical. So, either nothing is really physical or we do not really know what it is to be physical. This is often known as Hempel's Dilemma about what it is to be physical. So, thinking about it, it is no easy task to understand what it is to be physical.

More generally, as we saw in section 1, it is notoriously hard to define both the concrete and the abstract, even just to draw the line between them. So we should not dismiss the notion of metaphysical information, or information as reality, on the grounds that we understand the notions of being either concrete or abstract better, because arguably we do not. We must not confuse what we are accustomed to think and speak about and thereby assume we understand the nature of with what we really understand the nature of. Whether concrete and abstract objects ground information or information grounds concrete and abstract objects cannot be settled by merely claiming that one of them is better understood than the other.

What about information? Like with all more or less fundamental concepts, we should not expect a full analysis, with noncircular necessary and sufficient conditions, but there is in fact quite a bit we can say about the nature of (metaphysical) information. Importantly, there is a good ostensive explication of what it is. Information is *that which can be coded at one point, then transmitted to another point, where it can be decoded intact; whatever survives that process intact from beginning to end is information.* In a sense, information is thus simply that which survives a coding–decoding process. In the classic study of information theory, namely Shannon and Weaver (1949), we get the following five-part picture of communication of information. First, there is the *information source*, which selects a message out of a set of possible messages. Second, there is the *transmitter*, which codes up this message so that it can be sent through the communication channel from one point to another. Third, there is the *noise source*, which disturbs the message being transmitted. Fourth, there is the *receiver*, which decodes the message coming through the communication channel. Fifth, there is the *destination*, which receives the decoded message at the end point of the communication. Metaphysical information is *that which survives this process.* To the extent that the information going through this process remains intact at the end, there is successful communication of information.

For example, we can think of ourselves as information sources. We select a thought out of a set of many thoughts; we code it into a vocalizable language (transmitter); which we can utter as sound waves in the air, which moves from one person to another (communication channel); our ears and brain receive it, which we in turn decode into a thought (receiver); and then understand and receive (destination). There are many disturbances, for example, as the information moves through the air (noise source) but, to the degree our thought is the same thought at the beginning and end of this process, we have successfully communicated in the sense that information has been transferred from one person to another. Note that such communication does not only occur between persons but also between other kinds of living organisms, as well as between nonliving things, e.g. computers.

Metaphysical information can also be quantified (Shannon & Weaver, 1949; see also Stone, 2015). Roughly, one way to do that is to think of the amount of information as negative entropy. If we think of positive entropy as a state of disorder, then we can think of negative entropy as a state of order. Then, the amount of information is the amount of order, compared to a fixed background of possible disorder. For example, think of an on/off switch representing whether the light is on or off (respectively). Before we know whether the switch is on or off, the switch is, for us, in a state of disorder, in the sense that we have no information from that switch, but as soon as we know that the switch is (say) on, the switch is for us in a state of order, in the sense that we have full information from the switch. Generalizing, the amount of information is thus the amount of order in the sense of options ruled out, compared to a fixed background of possible options; i.e. the more information, the more order, the more options ruled out, the less entropy, the less uncertainty. The quantification of information can be made mathematically rigorous and noise can be minimized, which is the main reason for the success of today's ongoing digital revolution. Very naturally, we can measure information in terms of *bits* (binary digits; roughly, on/off switches) by virtue of the *logarithm function with base 2*: $\log_2 x = y$; where $\log_2 x = y$ is understood as equivalent with $2^y = x$. So, for example, the amount of information needed to choose one out of four options is 2 bits because $\log_2 4 = 2$ (i.e. $2^2 = 4$); likewise, the amount of information you need to choose one out of eight options is 3 bits, since $\log_2 8 = 3$ (i.e. $2^3 = 8$). The mathematical details need not concern us here, only the fact that they are well understood. Witnessed by today's digital technology, we have simply both theoretically and practically tamed information, which is another reason to think that information is a real thing and that there is a metaphysical nature to information to be studied.

I thus claim that the nature of information is not all that much less understood than the nature of the physical, the concrete, and the abstract. Again, we should not confuse what we are used to talk and think about with what we really understand. We might all be more used to talk and think about the abstract, concrete, and physical objects but I claim we do not thereby understand them all that much better than information. In fact, plausibly, we only understand the physical, concrete, and abstract in terms of the information we receive from it, even in the physical perceptual case. Of course, that is not saying that we understand the nature of information as well as we should. We definitely need to study it more; my claim is only that doing so is a promising project for better understanding the world and, ultimately, God.

One of the more interesting features of information, and an important one for our purposes, is that information seems to be independent of any particular medium to carry it. Recall, information is that which can be coded, transmitted from one point to another, and then decoded intact. This means that information can survive a transition through different media, which means it is independent of any particular one of them. Just think of a phone call and all the different media the information sent through a phone call can go through from beginning to end yet still remain intact. Even if it turns out to be the case that information is dependent on some medium or other, it is not dependent on any particular medium.

3.2 Informationalism

The thesis I will henceforth call *Informationalism* is the claim that, most fundamentally, reality is information. That is, most fundamentally, reality is the kind of thing that can be coded and then transmitted from one point to another, where it can be decoded intact.[6]

There are two distinct versions of informationalism in the vicinity. First, there is the more radical view that, most fundamentally, there is information independent of ("outside") any medium carrying it. Let us call this *pure informationalism* (PI). Second, there is the less radical view that, most fundamentally, there is information dependent on ("inside") a particular medium carrying it. Let us call this *impure informationalism* (II). Both PI and II claim that, most fundamentally, reality is information. According to PI, anything has its being in virtue of some of the information it carries and at the most fundamental level there is just pure information without any medium to carry it. According to II, anything has its being in virtue of some of the information it carries but there cannot be any information without a medium to carry it. In this picture, information needs some medium or other but no particular medium. In both pictures, information is fundamental in the sense that anything's being depends on some of the information it carries but the information it carries is independent of anything's being. For the purposes of this section, I will focus on the more radical PI, unless noted otherwise.

PI is thus an instance of what we might call *metaphysical monism*, which holds that, most fundamentally, reality is of one and only one sort. For comparison, think of another more popular instance of such metaphysical monism, namely the thesis of *physicalism*, which is the claim that, most fundamentally, reality is physical. Another example is the thesis of *concretism*, which is the claim that, most fundamentally, reality is concrete. Note that I am here thinking of it as a matter of metaphysical priority, not mere existence, so neither a physicalist nor a concretist need deny the existence of information, nor need an informationalist deny the existence of the physical or the concrete; rather a physicalist and a concretist need to explain how information is derived from the physical or the concrete and an informationalist needs to explain how the physical and the concrete are derived from information. I am not sure what a physicalist should say but an informationalist should say that being physical is communicating certain information to our senses.

---

[6] For more on the thesis of informationalism, see Bohn (n.d.).

For contrast, an example of metaphysical nonmonism (pluralism) is *dualism*, which is the claim that, most fundamentally, reality is both physical and mental. Another example of metaphysical nonmonism is the view that, most fundamentally, reality is both concrete and abstract, which is the kind of view that lies behind the problem of God and abstract objects. A general problem for any such metaphysical nonmonism is how to explain the interaction between the fundamental categories, e.g. how something mental can affect something physical or how something concrete can be affected by something abstract. Many are therefore tempted to go monistic. But a general problem for metaphysical monism is how to derive the other kinds of things from the one and only fundamental kind. For example, consider physicalism. A notorious problem is how to derive consciousness from physical matter. Consciousness is a first-person experience of what it is like to be in a state, which seems to be something categorically different from anything you find in a third-person nonexperiential physical language (a third-person description). Consciousness thus seems to go missing from the physical on not only practical but principal grounds. For another example, consider concretism. A notorious problem is not only how to derive the abstract from the concrete but also why we get so many abstract objects from comparatively so few concrete objects. For example, for any concrete object, there is not only one abstract object, namely its singleton set, but an infinity of sets built on top of it (the set of the set of the set of . . .). When we also think in terms of the powerset operation on these sets, we can in fact see higher orders of infinity, i.e. infinities of infinities, and so on. So, there are very, very many more abstract objects than concrete objects. One might think that the abstract is just creatures of our imagination but, since the mental is something concrete, we cannot locate all the abstract objects there are in the mental. So the question remains: How does it all arise from the concrete?

One way to try to solve such a problem, i.e. how to derive one category of things from another, is to go back to a form of metaphysical monism and look for a metaphysically deeper third category from which they both can be more easily derived than they can from each other. As an example in the case of how to derive the mental from the physical, we have the position of *neutral monism*. According to neutral monism, neither the physical nor the mental is derived from the other but both the physical and the mental derives from a nonphysical and nonmental kind of thing that underlies them both at a deeper metaphysical level. The main problem for neutral monism is of course that this third category is something we know not what is and hence neither do we know how to derive the physical and the mental from this we know not what is.

This is where informationalism carries more promise, both in the case of the physical/mental distinction and the concrete/abstract distinction. As we saw in section 3.1, we have a relatively firm grasp of what information is: We have an ostensive definition of it and we have mathematically rigorous ways to quantify it; in fact, we even have efficient physical ways to transmit it from A to B.

Here is one way to think of informationalism. Most fundamentally, reality is information. Information is that which can be coded and carried from one point to another, where it can be decoded intact. It is well known that there are many different ways of coding up the same information; today information is usually coded into a binary "language" but, in general, it is about switching the medium that carries the information for purposes of more efficiently processing that information but without loss of that very same information in the process. In our present picture, we take this idea further and claim that some information is coded abstractly and some is coded concretely; where some of the concrete information is coded as physical and some is coded as mental. To be coded concretely means something like being coded in a "language" that itself is in turn coded in such a way that it communicates the information we receive from all and only concrete things, i.e. tells us what it is to be concrete. Likewise, to be coded abstractly means something like being coded in a "language" that itself is in turn coded in such a way that it communicates the information we receive from all and only abstract things, i.e. tells us what it is to be abstract. So, in other words, the difference between the concrete and the abstract is a difference in the way information is coded. The nice thing about this picture is that there is no attempt to derive the abstract from the concrete (or vice versa), which has turned out to be really hard to understand how and why is supposed to happen. Rather, the concrete and the abstract are both derived from a third category of things, something they both have in common, namely information. And both kinds do carry information! For examples, there is a lot of information in the abstract structures of arithmetic and there is a lot of information in the concrete structures of human cells, so information can be coded both abstractly and concretely.

It might be tempting to think of information as something abstract but there are reasons to think that information is not reducible to the abstract and must therefore be something else altogether. For example, the same information can be gotten from different abstract structures, so that information cannot just be those abstract structures. For such an example, the same information we get out of Peano arithmetic can be gotten from different set-theoretical structures, so that very information cannot be identified or reduced to just one of the abstract structures. Information is multiply instantiated in abstract structures, as well as in concrete structures.

Interestingly, the same information we get from abstract structures can also be concretely encoded and instantiated. For example, we can program and make a computer perform (parts of) Peano arithmetic. The same information that we find in the abstract is then concretely coded and instantiated. What is common to it all is the very information that is differently coded and instantiated, both in the concrete and in the abstract. According to informationalism, it is that very information that is more fundamental than the abstract and concrete codings of it. The abstract and concrete are mere codings of the more fundamental information.

There is also another more abductive reason to resist thinking of information as something abstract. As we will soon see, informationalism is motivated by the fact that it provides great promise for solving many problems, e.g. the mind/body problem, not just the problem of God and abstract objects, which happens to be our concern here. But, if we identify information with something abstract, none of those problems will be solved. Their supposed solution rests on information being a fundamental category of its own. We must therefore assume that information is such a fundamental category of its own in order to see whether it can, as such, better explain or solve those problems. If it cannot, then we might go back to trying to understand it in terms of some other category, e.g. the abstract.

A most general (and classic-sounding) argument for informationalism is this: Information is independent of any particular kind of thing, witnessed by today's digital technology, where we code, process, and decode the same information in different media without loss. But no particular thing can exist or be anything without carrying any information whatsoever. So, even though information might be dependent on some medium or other, it is not dependent on any particular medium but any particular medium is dependent on carrying some information. Nothing can be anything without carrying some information. This indicates (but does not entail!) that information is more fundamental than any medium it might be carried in, including any abstract and concrete medium.

For a toy example, consider an electron. Let us assume, for simplicity, that an electron is simply that which has a certain mass m_e and negative charge c_n. Then, according to informationalism, an electron is most fundamentally the information carried (and coded) in $m_e + c_n$. In contrast, according to physicalism, an electron is most fundamentally the physical object that carries that information. As we saw, what that physical object is supposed to be is not all that easier to understand than what the information is supposed to be; in fact, thinking about it, the information we get from $m_e + c_n$ seems easier to grasp than the physical object carrying it. That the electron is physical is also just information communicated to us. The same goes for any physical object, as well as, in general, any concrete or abstract object.

A major worry for informationalism is how to best understand the idea that information gets coded in different ways, most notably physically versus mentally and concretely versus abstractly. That is, what does it mean for metaphysical information to be coded physically versus mentally and concretely versus abstractly? I believe the clue to an answer lies in how we receive information from physical things versus mental things and concrete things versus abstract things; but this problem needs much more work. I must here simply leave it at saying that I take this to be one of the more interesting future research areas when it comes to informationalism.

Admittedly, informationalism has a good old-fashioned Platonic smell to it. Plato famously thought that concrete objects are mere strivings to realize *the ideas* behind them, which are what really makes up fundamental reality. If we think of Plato's ideas as information, then informationalism is very close to Plato's original view. So, maybe informationalism is merely a contemporary version of good old-fashioned Platonism? I am not sure what Plato's position on ideas and abstract objects is but, for present purposes, it is important, as we saw earlier in this section, that informationalism does not identify information with abstract objects. According to informationalism, information is its own kind of thing, transcending both the abstract and the concrete. Information is what both kinds encode in different ways. But if informationalism is in fact close to Plato's original view, I say all the more power to good old Plato!

Recall, I am here thinking of PI. If, on the other hand, we think of impure informationalism, then we get a view seemingly closer to Aristotle's immanent ideas than Plato's transcendent ideas.

I realize that informationalism might seem radical to some, and that it needs much more thought than what we can give it here, but sometimes deep problems require radical solutions. In fact, informationalism carries great promise to solve many deep problems, not just the problem of God and abstract objects (to which we shortly turn). There is thus an abductive argument in the vicinity here. To the extent informationalism can better solve these deeper problems than its rivals, we should believe informationalism. This is not the place to discuss all such problems but let me just all too briefly end this section by all to briefly mentioning two such problems, in addition to the problem of God and abstract objects to be discussed in the next section. First, it carries promise to solve the notorious mind/body problem or what is today often construed as a physical/conscious problem. As Chalmers (1996, chap. 8) speculates, information might be what links consciousness with physical reality. It might merely be two ways of coding the same information. Informationalism might also provide the answer to neutral monism's big question: What kind of thing is it that underlies both the physical and the mental? Information! Again, it might be that the physical and the mental (or consciousness) are just two different ways of encoding, implementing, and processing information.

Second, informationalism carries promise to solve some interesting epistemological problems. For example, how is it that we physical human beings can gain knowledge of abstract mathematical structures (see Benacerraf, 1973)? One might speculate that a concrete human being can gain knowledge of an abstract structure by concretely coding the same information as what is coded by the abstract structure. In other words, our concrete thoughts and language can code the same information as that which is coded in abstract mathematical structures (though, of course, we do not code all of it) and we can thus gain mathematical knowledge of the same information (assuming the coding is reliable, safe, justified, or whatever is needed for knowledge). In other words, mathematical knowledge is not had by, e.g., causal interaction but by coding and individuating information as found in mathematical truths. (For another interesting use of the notion of information to better understand knowledge, see Dretske, 1981.)

I believe there are many other traditional philosophical problems that informationalism can help us better understand but a discussion of them must be for another time. In this Element, we are only interested in informationalism to the extent it can help us solve the problem of God and abstract objects, to which we now finally turn.

3.3 Divine Informationalism

The thesis of *Divine Informationalism* (DI) is the claim that God is the fundamental information from which all other things derive their being. As with PI and II in section 3.2, there are two possible positions here. One is that God is information "inside" some medium or other (though not dependent on any one of them) and another is that God is information "outside" any medium. As Tillich (1973) famously points out, God cannot be just another object among all other objects but must be something very special, so I will henceforth work on the assumption that God is information "outside" any medium, independent of all of them. As per the theses of DF and aseity, God is thus all and only pure information, the source of all other things, hirself independent of any medium to carry it.

Note that there is again another slightly different position in the neighborhood according to which, most fundamentally, reality is God but God hirself is not pure information but creates the rest of reality by encoding information in both abstract and concrete ways. Dembski (2014) seems to defend such a position. But the problem for our purposes is that it seems to raise an analogous problem to the problem of God and abstract objects that we discuss and try to solve in this Element. Nothing can ever fully lack information. Whatever exists carries some information. So, God, in order to exist at all, carries some information. Just like God cannot exist without instantiating hir nature, so God cannot exist without carrying some information. Yet if information is distinct from God, but modally and temporally coextensional with God, this creates the exact analog of the problem of God and abstract objects we started out with; we might call it *the problem of God and information*.

To solve that problem, or not get it in the first place, a theist should think of God hirself as pure information. In a sense, instead of identifying God with hir nature, I suggest identifying God with fundamental information. If God's nature is a set of essential properties, then, according to DI, since God is pure information, which is reducible to neither objects nor properties, God has no nature; God is just pure information and we must resist the temptation to try to fully understand that in terms of objects or properties. Information is its own kind of fundamental category. Recall information is that which can be coded and transmitted from A to B, where it can be decoded intact. Unfortunately, there is no way to grasp pure information and hence no way to grasp God, except through coding and decoding, but that does not mean that God is most fundamentally of the form of our coding and decoding. God is not the code but that which is coded.

Yet God is supposed to be a personal being worthy of worship, so the divine information must be a personal kind of information; I say, most likely a conscious and normative kind of information. We cannot fully dig into this here but note that the notion of metaphysical information, or information as reality, does not rule out it being a personal, conscious, and normative kind of information. Maybe fundamental information and fundamental consciousness/normativity come to the same thing. Even if God created the world by encoding some information abstractly and some concretely, some of which in turn is physical and some of it mental, and thus communicates with us, the initial divine pure information, the source of it all, might still be a personal, conscious, and normative kind of information without itself most fundamentally being either concrete or abstract. The metaphysical categories of concrete and abstract might be just two different kinds of information, coded by the fundamental informational God, for us to try to decode, for whatever (seemingly inscrutable!) reasons God might have in mind. The reason a theist should think of God as a concrete personal being comes from decoding the information communicated to us.

DI seems to help solve many of our problems with respect to God and abstract objects. First of all, consider the grounding problem, how a necessary and eternal concrete God can ground necessary and eternal abstract objects. By adopting DI, the problem seems to rest on a mistaken presupposition of there being a fundamental distinction between concrete and abstract objects, with God being on the concrete side. According to DI, there is no such fundamental distinction but rather God is pure (personal, conscious, and normative) information that encodes some of hir information in terms of abstract objects and some of it in terms of concrete objects, for us to decode. So the way God grounds abstract and concrete objects is by a way of coding information. That some things are abstract and others are concrete is just more information for us to receive. We should thus, at least for present purposes, switch focus from trying to understand grounding to trying to understand ways of coding or, in the case at hand, trying to understand grounding in terms of coding. The direction of priority is given by the direction of coding: God codes abstract and concrete objects; abstract and concrete objects do not code God. This direction is no more mysterious than the direction of coding elsewhere, e.g. where I code a computer program without that computer program coding me.

The fact that abstract objects are necessary and eternal things might then just mean that God instantaneously coded it all as a presupposition for any concrete coding. That means simply that all the information God concretely coded presupposes all the information God abstractly coded, but not vice versa. Another way of putting it is that the concrete is simply a differently coded proper substructure of the abstract and the way the concrete processes information, i.e. the algorithmic information for the concrete, cannot go beyond the information in the abstract. As a theoretical bonus, that also helps make sense of how and why mathematized science works so well in understanding and manipulating the concrete world. This is another way of understanding Morris and Menzel's (1986) idea that we cannot step outside of the created modal space we are a part of.

One might also further speculate that semantic information, i.e. information about things, presupposes that the most fundamental informational source is a personal, conscious, and normative kind of information and hence that the latter might help explain the former. But again, we cannot go into that here; it must be left for future research.

Second, consider the bootstrapping problem, how God can ground hir own nature. The problem simply dissolves. According to DI, there is no need for the 3D printer analogy we considered earlier because there is no difference between God and hir nature, because there is no fundamental distinction between objects and properties. The bootstrapping problem thus never arises to begin with. God is not an object with some properties; rather, God is pure information, at least part of which can be coded in terms of objects and properties and thus transmitted to us for purposes of communication. So God does not create hir own nature á la the analogy of the 3D printer; a better analogy is that God codes a computer program for the concrete world to play out, a program that presupposes certain abstractly coded objects and, in that program, some of hir information is encoded in terms of those abstract and concrete objects and properties that we can decode in a way we (partly) understand. That is how we can gain knowledge.

Again, we must resist the temptation to try to reduce God to talk of objects or properties. That is, we must resist the temptation to say that God must have had some properties prior to coding any of hir information, e.g. the capacity to code. According to DI, objects and properties are coded information, so any talk of God's properties prior to hir coding of any information can only, at best, be made sense of posterior to hir coding of some of hir information. God hirself is pure information, which can only be referred to ostensively but be coded in many different ways, objects and properties being only two such ways. God hirself is prior to any such coding of objects and properties, which is why there is no bootstrapping problem.

I am of course not claiming that DI solves all our problems, with no problems of its own. DI is still too obscure as is. I am only claiming that it carries great promise, worth serious philosophical attention, certainly more than it has gotten so far (for some rare but promising exceptions, see e.g. Dembski, 2014; Ward, 2014). In any case, let it at least be an interesting suggestion for more future research in the philosophy of religion (and metaphysics!).

3.4 Divine Concreteness?

Let me end this Element with yet another loosely connected idea for future research. In sections 1.1–1.2, I claimed that to be abstract is to not be concrete and one way to try to understand what it means to be concrete is to be determinate, where something is determinate if and only if for any property it either has it or it has its negation (and it never has both and it never has neither). This understanding of the distinction makes being concrete a limit-point, with being abstract a matter of degree away from being concrete. The less determinate you are, the less concrete you are, the more abstract you are.

We should keep the notion of something being *vague* apart from this particular notion of something being nondeterminate, or indeterminate, that is meant to capture being abstract. I take vagueness as a matter of semantic indecision (see Lewis, 1986), others take it to be a matter of epistemic ignorance (Williamson, 1996), but I will here simply assume none of us should take it to be a matter of metaphysical reality. That is, when the boundaries of an object are vague this is because no one has settled where to draw the line or we just do not know where to draw it; it is never a matter of metaphysical reality. But being abstract is a metaphysical matter of reality, not a matter of semantic indecision or epistemic ignorance. It is impossible to make an abstract object concrete by making a semantic decision, neither does it go from abstract to concrete by anyone gaining more knowledge.

So the fact that concrete objects can seem vague but abstract objects seem nonvague is neither here nor there for our purposes of drawing the concrete/abstract distinction in terms of being determinate.

On this way of understanding what it is to be concrete, there is a striking potential connection between concreteness and information; it might even help us better understand the relationship between, on the one hand, God as pure information and, on the other hand, the rest of reality as concretely and abstractly coded information. As we saw in section 3.1, information can be thought of as negative entropy, meaning that, the less uncertainty, the more information, in the sense of, the more options are ruled out, the more information. But being concrete is being such that all open options of properties are ruled out; you either have a property or you do not, for *any* property. So concrete things are the most informational with respect to properties and always more informational than abstract things. What we can or do know about an object is irrelevant here; being concrete is already having ruled out one of two options with respect to any property, so there is no uncertainty left in the sense of such open options. Being abstract, on the other hand, is not having ruled out one of two options with respect to all property, so there is uncertainty left in the sense of some such open options.

For example, consider you and me. We are very concrete things. If we ask the question of who weighs the most, you or me, there is a definite answer. Either you weigh more than me, the same as me, or less than me. But consider my singleton set and me. If we ask the question of who weighs the most of my singleton set and me, there is seemingly no answer. One might be tempted to answer that it weighs the same as me but it is more (at least equally) tempting to answer that the singleton set is a kind of object for which weight makes no sense. A singleton set has no weight; not in the sense of weighing 0 kg but in the sense of weight not applying to it at all. Abstract sets are not apt for weight. The same might go for many other properties, e.g. color, shades, causal powers, and spatiotemporal location. With respect to me, there is an answer, but with respect to my singleton set there might not be an answer when it comes to such properties. By our definitions above, that is what makes the singleton set abstract, presumably more so than me.

The degree of abstractness of something might then simply be measured by the degree of open options with respect to whether it has a property F, for any

F; that is, its abstractness can be directly read off the amount of information it carries with respect to properties. The more entropy, the less options ruled out, the more abstract; the less entropy, the more options ruled out, the more concrete.

As suggested in section 1, arguably, I am at least somewhat abstract, not fully concrete. For example, I am human; being human is part of what it is to be me. But where is my humanity spatiotemporally located? How big a part of me is my humanity? How much does it weigh? Such questions seem to have no answer because the properties involved do not apply to my humanity at all; the questions seem to rest on a category mistake. So I am partly an abstract object, though I am much more concrete than, say, the prime number three.

But then what, if anything, can be fully concrete? An interesting thesis is that the one and only fully concrete being is God, call this the thesis of *Divine Concreteness* (DC). The idea would be that God is not only the most fundamental being there can be but also the most fundamental information, or the most informational being, there can be and, as such, by virtue of the above idea of concreteness being measured by determinateness, or how much information it carries with respect to properties, God would thereby also be the most concrete being there can be. God would be the one and only fully concrete being, or the limit-point of concreteness.

One might object that there seem to be some properties not applying to God at all, just like is the case with us, hence making God less than fully concrete. For example, spatiotemporal location, darkness, as well as mass and color just do not seem to apply to God. But, if that is so, then, in this picture, God is also partly abstract. Perhaps God is even more abstract than we are.

There are ways out of this problem. One might simply bite the bullet and hold that, for any property, God has either it or its negation. After all, God is a special kind of being. For example, perhaps God does have a spatiotemporal location as well as a mass and color. Perhaps God is located everywhere and hir mass is the mass of the entire universe and hir darkness and color are the darkness and color distribution of the entire universe. This amounts to forms of pantheism (roughly, that God is in nature) or panentheism (roughly, that nature is in God). Or perhaps, for any spatiotemporal location, God is not located there; for any color, God does not have that color; and, with respect to mass, perhaps God either has no mass or infinite mass. In any case, in some such picture, God is apt for all properties and, for any property, God has either it or its negation, making hir the most concrete thing there can be.

Alternatively, one might hold that concreteness is like height in the sense that nothing is fully tall but only more or less tall relative to other things; height has no top level. One might then hold that God is the most concrete thing there can be, without anything being fully concrete.

As in section 1.2, the problem is of course to find a system for such overall measurement. But, given some of the things that have been suggested in this Element, it is another interesting thought worth thinking about if you believe that God is the concrete foundation of all there is and can be.

Concluding Remarks

In section 1, we looked at different versions of the problem of God and abstract objects and ended up with what I take to be the most interesting and fundamental version of it, namely what I called the grounding problem. In section 2, we looked at various kinds of solutions to it and ended up with what I take to be the most interesting and plausible solution to it, namely divine conceptualism, where the abstract objects are grounded in God's mind. In section 3, we looked at a different and somewhat new approach that rejects the basic presupposition of the problem as it is discussed in sections 1 and 2, namely that reality is most fundamentally populated by objects and properties. According to this new approach, reality is most fundamentally pure information, independent of any medium to carry it.

Much of this Element has been more suggestive than conclusive. I have also taken many shortcuts and made more or less unjustifiably personal priorities. For example, I spent too little energy on arguing for the grounding problem in favor of the other versions of the problem. For instance, I should have spent more energy on the notion of creation at an instant. I also spent too little energy on the alternatives of rejecting the existence of either God or abstract objects, in favor of perhaps spending too much energy on the alternative of DI. When it comes to informationalism, and DI, more energy should be spent on the notions of coding up, implementing, processing, and decoding information and especially on what it is for information to be coded concretely (and physically) versus abstractly. The big remaining question is of course also what it is for God to be pure information independently of any medium.

I encourage the reader to dig into these matters in much more detail. In the meantime, I hope that this Element at least has been somewhat interesting, engaging, and inspiring for purposes of more research.

References

Adriaans, P. (2018). Information. In E. N. Zalta (ed.), *Stanford Encyclopedia of Philosophy.* https://plato.stanford.edu/archives/win2018/entries/information/

Aisawa, K. & Gillett, C. (eds.) (2016). *Scientific Composition and Metaphysical Ground.* Palgrave Macmillan.

Barnes, E. (2018). Symmetric dependence. As in Bliss & Priest (eds.) (2018).

Beaney, M. (ed.) (1997). *The Frege Reader.* Blackwell.

Benacerraf, P. (1973). Mathematical truth. *Journal of Philosophy,* 70(19), 661–679.

Bergmann, M. & Brower, J. (2006). A theistic argument against Platonism (and in support of truthmakers and divine simplicity). As in Zimmerman (ed.) (2006).

Bliss, R. & Priest, G. (eds.). (2018). *Reality and Its Structure: Essays in Fundamentality.* Oxford University Press.

Bliss, R. & Trogdon, K. (2014). Metaphysical grounding. In E. N. Zalta (ed.), *Stanford Encyclopedia of Philosophy.* https://plato.stanford.edu/archives/win2016/entries/grounding/

Bohn, E. D. (2012). Anselmian theism and indefinitely extensible perfection. *Philosophical Quarterly,* 62(249), 671–683.

(2017). Divine necessity. *Philosophy Compass,* 12(11). https://onlinelibrary.wiley.com/doi/abs/10.1111/phc3.12457

(2018a). Indefinitely descending ground. As in Bliss & Priest (eds.) (2018).

(2018b). Divine foundationalism. *Philosophy Compass,* 13(10). https://onlinelibrary.wiley.com/doi/abs/10.1111/phc3.12524

(n.d.). Informationalism. (Paper in progress.)

Burgess, J. & Rosen, G. (1997). *A Subject Without an Object: Strategies for the Nominalistic Interpretation of Mathematics.* Oxford University Press.

Chalmers, D. J. (1996). *The Conscious Mind: In Search of a Fundamental Theory.* Oxford University Press.

Chalmers, D., Manley, D., & Wasserman, R. (eds.) (2009). *Metametaphysics.* Oxford University Press.

Cowling, S. (2017). *Abstract Entities.* Routledge.

Craig, W. L. (2012). Nominalism and divine aseity. As in Kvanvig (ed.) (2012).

(2014). Anti-Platonism. As in Gould (ed.) (2014).

(2017). *God and Abstract Objects.* Springer.

Davies, P. & Gregersen, N. H. (eds.) (2014). *Information and the Nature of Reality.* Cambridge University Press.

Davison, S. A. (1991). Could abstract objects depend upon God? *Religious Studies*, 27(4), 485–497.

Dembski, W. A. (2014). *Being as Communion: A Metaphysics of Information*. Routledge.

Descartes, R. (1630). Letter to Mersenne. In *The philosophical writings of Descartes Volume III*. Edited by John Cottingham et al. Cambridge University Press, 1991.

Dretske, F. (1981). *Knowledge and the Flow of Information*. MIT Press.

Fine, K. (2001). The question of realism. *Philosopher's Imprint*, 1(1), 1–30.

Floridi, L. (2011). *The Philosophy of Information*. Oxford University Press.

Fowler, G. (2015). Simplicity or priority? As in Kvanvig (ed.) (2015).

Frege, G. (1918). Thought. As in Beaney (ed.) (1997).

Gould, P. M. (2014a). Can God create abstract objects? A reply to Peter van Inwagen. *Sophia*, 53(1), 99–112.

Gould, P. M. (ed.) (2014b). *Beyond the Control of God? Six Views on the Problem of God and Abstract Objects*. Bloomsbury.

Hale, B. & Hoffman, A. (eds.) (2010). *Modality*. Oxford University Press.

Kvanvig, J. L. (2015). *Oxford Studies in Philosophy of Religion*, Vol. 6. Oxford University Press.

(2012). *Oxford Studies in Philosophy of Religion*, Vol, 4. Oxford University Press.

Leftow, B. (1990). Is God an abstract object? *Noûs*, 24(4), 581–598.

(2012). *God and Necessity*. Oxford University Press.

Lewis, D. (1986). *On the Plurality of Worlds*. Blackwell.

Morris, T. V. & Menzel, C. (1986). Absolute creation. *American Philosophical Quarterly*, 23(4), 353–362.

Nagasawa, Y. (2008). A new defense of Anselmian theism. *Philosophical Quarterly*, 58, 577–596.

(2017). *Maximal God: A New Defense of Perfect Being Theism*. Oxford University Press.

Plantinga, A. (1980). *Does God Have a Nature?* Marquette University Press.

Raven, M. (2015). Ground. *Philosophy Compass*,10(15).

Rosen, G. (2010). Metaphysical dependence: Grounding and reduction. As in Hale et al. (eds.) (2010).

Schaffer, J. (2009). On what grounds what. As in Chalmers et al (eds.) (2009).

(2010). Monism: the priority of the whole. *Philosophical Review*, 119:1, pp. 31–76.

(2016a). Ground rules: Lessons from Wilson. As in Aisawa & Gillett (eds.) (2016).

(2016b). Grounding in the image of causation. *Philosophical Studies,* Vol.173, pp.49–100.

Shannon, C. E. & Weaver, W. (1949). *The Mathematical Theory of Communication.* University of Illinois Press.

Stone, J. V. (2015). *Information Theory: A tutorial introduction.* Sebtel Press.

Tillich, P. (1973). *Systematic Theology,* Vol. 1. University of Chicago Press.

Timpe, K. (ed.) (2009). *Metaphysics and God: Essays in Honor of Eleonore Stump.* Routledge.

van Inwagen, P. (2004). A theory of properties. As in van Inwagen (2014).

(2009). God and other uncreated things. As in Timpe, K. (ed.) (2009).

(2014). *Existence: Essays in Ontology.* Cambridge University Press.

(2015). Did God create shapes? *Philosophia Christi,* 17(2), 285–290.

Ward, K. (2014). God as the ultimate informational principle. As in Davies & Gregersen (eds.) (2014).

Welty, G. (2014). Theistic conceptual realism. As in Gould (ed.) (2014b).

Williamson, T. (1996). *Vagueness.* Routledge.

(2013). *Modal Logic as Metaphysics.* Oxford University Press.

Zimmerman, D. W. (ed.) (2006). *Oxford Studies in Metaphysics,* Vol. 2. Oxford University Press.

Acknowledgments

I would like to thank everyone with whom I have discussed the topics of this book at some point or other but, especially, Matti Eklund, Paul Gould, Atle Ottesen Søvik, and Kelly Trogdon for discussions and comments. I would also like to thank the series editor Yujin Nagasawa and my wife Karen Duenger, without whom this book would never have happened.

This Element is dedicated to Bork, Ask, and Yme.

Cambridge Elements ☰

Philosophy of Religion

Yujin Nagasawa

University of Birmingham

Yujin Nagasawa is Professor of Philosophy and Co-Director of the John Hick Centre for Philosophy of Religion at the University of Birmingham. He is currently President of the British Society for the Philosophy of Religion. He is a member of the Editorial Board of *Religious Studies*, the *International Journal for Philosophy of Religion* and *Philosophy Compass*.

About the Series

This Cambridge Elements series provides concise and structured introductions to all the central topics in the philosophy of religion. It offers balanced, comprehensive coverage of multiple perspectives in the philosophy of religion. Contributors to the series are cutting-edge researchers who approach central issues in the philosophy of religion. Each provides a reliable resource for academic readers and develops new ideas and arguments from a unique viewpoint.

Cambridge Elements ≡

Philosophy of Religion